THE REAL ALE RAMBLER

QUAFFING ALONG THE NORFOLK COAST PATH

NEIL COLLINGS

BANNISTER
PUBLICATIONS

First published in Great Britain in 2024 by
Bannister Publications Ltd
2A Market Hall, Chesterfield, Derbyshire, S40 1AR

Copyright © Neil Collings 2024

ISBN: 978-1-916823-19-8

A catalogue record for this book is available from the British Library

Typeset by Bannister Publications Ltd
Cover illustrations by Gregg Hardy

Printed and bound by CMP UK Ltd, in Great Britain

This book was self-published by Bannister Publications.
For more information on self-publishing visit:
www.bannisterpublications.com

CONTENTS

Along the Norfolk Coast Path	1
Introduction	4
Hunstanton to Burnham Deepdale	19
Burnham Deepdale to Stiffkey	37
Stiffkey to Salthouse	60
Sheringham to Cromer	85
Salthouse to Sheringham	112
Hopton on Sea to California Cliffs	127
Scratby to Happisburgh	157
Happisburgh to Overstrand	181
Overstrand to Cromer	210
The Real Ale Rambler - Roll of Honour	221

ALONG THE NORFOLK COAST PATH

It's all so (Le) Strange in 'Sunny Hunny'
While there's a dose of the Blues in Stiffkey
They're minding the Gap along the beach at Holkham
Pilgrims for St John the Baptist at the parish church,
Trimingham
Wells next the Sea for the heritage Maltings
Is it Sea Palling, Pawling or even perhaps Pauling?
Fish & Chips, an ice cream then playing the slots at
Hemsby
You'll find Hope at Weybourne when visiting the Priory
Windswept Marshes and the iconic Windmill at Cley
Watch Sidestrand's Biplane Bomber, soaring high
They say the NILA 'Never Turn Back' at Caister
Search for gold coins among the Cliffs of California
Landmine Memorial outside the museum in Mundesley

What's the Point? A ten-minute walk from the quayside,
Blakeney

If you happen to like Barns there's the Great one at Waxham
And also the old Coal Barn on the edge of the marshes,
Thornham

Fishermen, with their catch, Return to the sanctuary of
Winterton

An albatross keeps watch over the Ancient Mariner in Old
Hunstanton

A bronze age Sea Henge was uncovered at Holme next
the Sea

Shannocks of Sheringham for the musical Men of Shanty
Visit the Branodunum Roman Fort of Brancaster
Off the Downs at Morston, before carefully dropping the
Anchor

There's basking Seals galore all along the beach at Horsey
Approaching Burnham Deepdale there's more than one
Sailor who's Jolly

Look down onto the stunning sandy beach from the Grand
Old Prom, Gorleston

In 1990 a fossilised skeleton of a mammoth was discovered
in West Runton

Haisbro' proudly has both a Hill House and a candy cane
Lighthouse

Mercifully escaping the shingle for a recuperative pint at
the Dun Cow, Salthouse

Devour a yummy brownie or scrumptious sausage roll at Scratby Bakery

Holding out for a Hero near the Staithe in Burnham Overy

Great Yarmouth boasts a choice of Piers and the (now) rare delicacy of Bloaters

Visit Hopton on Sea to watch the World Indoor Bowls championship at Potters

And finally, saunter along Cromer Pier…then up the steps to the Red Lion for a celebratory beer!

Neil Collings (October 2023)

INTRODUCTION

Hands up then. Who has ever comprehensively and painstakingly planned a major event only to wake up on that very first morning in a cold sweat, eyes wide open, glaring at the bedroom ceiling in a fixated and panicked manner? Realisation has uncomfortably started to kick in with the mind working overtime. 'I've bitten off more than I can chew here' or 'If I manage to complete this successfully it will be one of my greatest achievements' or more pertinently 'Why the fuck do I put myself through this'. During preparation and on paper things look brilliantly achievable don't they, in reality not so much so.

But wait. I'm not talking about the physical challenge of walking 84 miles along the Norfolk Coast

Path here, by the way. I'm talking about the proposed five railway journeys, plus one bus, to get my daughter (the adorable Alisha, aka Leesh or Leeshy) and I, to the path's starting point at Hunstanton. You see, according to the East Midlands Railway (EMR) website the first recommended train out of my hometown of Chesterfield to get us to King's Lynn was scheduled to be at midday and, historically being the possessor of extremely itchy feet, I needed to find a solution that would get us 'out of the traps' a lot earlier in the day. Thus, the booking of the intricately linked five train services as follows:

Depart Chesterfield 08:06 / Arrive Sheffield 08:19
Depart Sheffield 08:36 / Arrive Doncaster 09:02
Depart Doncaster 09:20 / Arrive Peterborough 10:06
Depart Peterborough 10:19 / Arrive Ely 10:53
Depart Ely 11:22 / Arrive King's Lynn 11:53

I know what's going through your head and I have to agree. 'Utter madness Neil. What on earth were you thinking'. It's basically the equivalent of having a five-team accumulator on the football coupon – there's always one of the blighters that lets you down isn't there (usually MK Dons FC if you're asking).

So, rather early one beautiful and sunny Sunday morning in May 2023 we set off on our travels, the bright-eyed optimism and excitement of starting our East Anglian hike tempered with the knowledge that there were to be several train-shaped hoops to jump through before reaching our initial destination of 'Sunny Hunny', that west facing seaside resort on the east coast (are you keeping up at the back?). Chesterfield railway station had its usual eclectic mix of early morning dwellers in attendance; a subtle blend of travellers keen to get on their way (like us), train spotters eager to see that elusive freight engine, plus a few people who were obviously suffering the after-effects of a substantial night out on the town. This latter category included one youngish chap who was diligently attempting to pebble dash the whole of the pavement with the highly noxious combination of Jägermeister, kebab meat and probably other substances that may not be readily available over the counter at your local supermarket. Unperturbed by the dubious quality of ad-hoc entertainment being provided, Alisha and I settled on having the customary departure photo from this neck of the woods by standing alongside the bronze statue of George Stephenson at the front of the station concourse; the famous steam railway engineer looking for all the world like he was giving the whole of Derbyshire an impressively elongated middle finger. He's not, it's the funnel from a model of

'Locomotion No.1' that he is displaying with his left hand.

Regarding the first part of our journey, I'm pleased to report that Chesterfield to Sheffield went smoothly, Sheffield to Donny likewise. "Piece of piss this railway travel isn't it Leeshy" I blustered, clicking my heels in Gene Kelly 'Singing in the Rain' fashion while giving myself a good old congratulatory pat on the back in a rather excessive show of self-adulation. "I don't know why I was fretting."

"Daaaaaad" muttered a hesitant Alisha, tentatively pointing towards the departure boards. "It says there are three trains, including ours, all scheduled to arrive on platform 3A at the same time of 09:20." She was right. They were all heading for King's Cross and included the delayed 08:23 LNER service (due to stop at Peterborough), the delayed 09:11 Grand Central service (not stopping at Peterborough) and the on-time 09:20 LNER service (also due to stop at Peterborough). Now at this point I must own up to not being an expert in platform allocation but what I do know is that it's bloody impossible for three great big inter-city units to arrive at the same place at the same time. Panic and confusion were the staples to be found amongst our fellow commuters, resembling a scene from Doctor Who where everyone has been indoctrinated by some sort of alien nerve gas preventing them from thinking straight. They were banging into each other, cracking each other's shins with hefty suitcases, poking each other in the eye with stray hiking sticks (that may have been Leeshy), going around in circles, hands up in the air in despair, not one person with any idea what to do, wailing like banshees. And yes, that did include the railway staff who were there to guide us.

By now even the first of those three trains was over 60 minutes late, meaning if we were to catch the one that we had booked we were sure to miss our connection later down the line to Ely. I told you there was always one didn't I? But I had a cunning plan…

When the now seriously delayed 08:23 service finally limped to a halt I said "Quick Leesh, follow me" as I navigated through the bamboozled throng for the rear carriage. A beleaguered and yet testy-looking guard jumped down onto the heaving platform. Here we had one seriously grumpy fellow. As he agitatedly dabbed his sweaty brow with his shirt sleeve I very politely (and bravely for me) enquired "Excuse me please. My daughter and I have tickets booked on the 09:20 train to Peterborough, but if we wait for that service to arrive I fear we'll miss our onward connections to King's Lynn. Is there any chance we can hop on this one instead?" optimistically proffering our tickets so he could validate them.

He glared at said tickets, then glowered at me, snapping "What makes you think you can catch this train? Yours is in an hours' time. No way."

"Well, it's not really in an hour is it?" I cautiously retorted, obviously risking a battering in doing so. "The time is nearly half 9 so we're already delayed aren't we?"

After having another cursory check of the tickets (while also wanting to get his train out of Doncaster as quickly as possible) he scowled at me before acknowledging "OK. On this occasion I'll allow you on. BUT DON'T MAKE A HABIT OF IT."

'Grrrrrrrr...bloody customers...tossers' I could imagine him chuntering as the whistle blew to signal our departure. But we didn't care as we were back on our travels eastwards.

Once inside the carriage it was a sight to behold. Later on that day, in the capital, West Ham were scheduled to play Leeds in a Premier League football fixture. Both sets of fans, mainly singular and not in the usual leery and obnoxious groups that we're accustomed to seeing on the rail network, were harmoniously journeying south alongside each either. It reminded me of the dog situation within public houses across the land, you know, the one where there is a canine resting under the majority of each of the tables as their respective human view their mobiles or does a crossword. Each dog appears to be well behaved and under control and yet you know they are all fully aware of each other's existence, they've seen each other over the weeks and months and studied each other out of the corner of their eye, making sure that one of the others doesn't receive more pub treats than they do. They instinctively know that if they, individually, were to bark and cause a scene they could possibly be taken home in disgrace, never to return, with no more enjoyable and lucrative visits to hoover up the discarded peanuts and crisps. It is, of course, totally acceptable for them to all aggressively stand up and bark in unison if an unknown dog walks in, thus affecting the doggy 'feng shui'.

Bizarrely, the two sets of fans were conducting themselves in a remarkably similar fashion. None of the usual posturing and dullard behaviour here. Replica club shirts were noticeable, they knew who each other were, knew where each other were sat, secretly glancing as a member of the opposition walked down the aisle. But there was no animosity and certainly no aggression. For people with experience of how these two teams' supporters have behaved in times gone by it would be a total revelation to observe. Just like the dogs in the pub it was as if they knew that if they misbehaved then they could be thrown off the train, maybe banned from the rail network, ultimately missing this match and probably a few more into the bargain.

As I tucked into my first can of beer of the day (us athletes do need to keep hydrated after all) I spotted that a lot of them were drinking water and/or coffee! I know, I know - do you think it will ever catch on?

You'll be relieved to find out that we arrived in King's Lynn without any further alarm or delay. For those of you with an unhealthy fetish for station monuments (and these people are amongst us) you'll be delighted to find out that this northern terminus of the Fen line is due to have its own in the near future. It promises to be an absolute belter as well and it's all to do with the 'Brotherhood of the Grey Goose Feather'. 'What's all that about then Neil', I hear you ask. Well thanks for enquiring. Hundreds of years ago, before the low-lying peatlands of the Fens were banked and drained, there was a secret fellowship of the grey goose feather. The locals, who grafted a living from the marshland and water, would carry a feather from the grey goose that was split in two and when in need they would present it. Any fellow true Fenlander would be obliged to assist them. Their motto was *'I am a fenlander, a true fenlander. All true folk of this area carry this token and if in need are sworn to help, unto even their own death, another who carries a grey goosefeather'.*

Just like with intricately linked train services and

five-team accumulators on the football coupon there is always one to let the side down (even in brotherhoods) and in this instance it just happened to be the most famous Puritanical MP and East Anglian skirmisher of them all. The website, Tales from the Fen, explains *'During the English Civil war a publican, by the name of Mucky Porter, helped the King to cross the treacherous fenland to escape from Oliver Cromwell. When asked by the court to prove he could be trusted with this task Mucky produced a grey goose feather and cut it in half, explaining that this was a sign of a true Fenlander and that all who produced this token could be guaranteed help in their hour of need. When the party arrived at Huntingdon they were met by Oliver Cromwell's men but when they produced their goose feathers they were let to pass. As you may well know King Charles was eventually captured by Oliver Cromwell and on the eve of his execution he is said to have presented Cromwell with a split grey goose feather. This is said to have caused Cromwell much anguish but as history will tell us King Charles was executed the very next day. But when the Fenlanders in Cromwell's army got word of this they threw their feathers at Cromwell's feet and refused to follow him any longer'.*

The steel artwork (depicting one of the feathers), designed by Annabel McCourt and Adrian Riley, was to be split into two 8ft halves that would appear to merge as travellers moved around them, offering a warm welcome to the town and friendship for life. Isn't that great! I certainly look forward to seeing it at a later visit to this part of West Norfolk.

All that was left for us to do now was catch the No. 36 Coastliner bus to Old Hunstanton (I say 'all that was left' casually – there's potentially 38 stops on the journey) from the King's Lynn transport interchange. Digs had been booked at the Wash & Tope pub in Hunstanton as we wanted to be as close as possible to the waymarker indicating the start of the Norfolk Coast Path the following morning. Yet after extensive research it was apparent that the town was not a great advert for real ale. Old Hunstanton however, the very scenic and more quieter village sibling a mile and a half up the road, did contain an intriguing establishment called the Mariner Inn.

An hour later, after a pleasant, meandering journey that trundled through picturesque villages including Dersingham, Ingoldisthorpe and Snettisham – the trio sounding for all the world like a firm of rather dodgy solicitors – we arrived. The Mariner (previously known as the Ancient Mariner) on first inspection from the roadside appeared to be a very old inn indeed. However, records show that it was strangely not a pub until as relatively recently as 1984. Predominantly built from flint and brick, this sprawling building dates back to the 1600's and is an amalgamation of barns plus the stable block for the adjacent building, the Le Strange Hotel. Once inside you'll find oak beams aplenty atop low ceilings, quarry tiled flooring plus an interesting collection of local nautical prints and regalia. You also get the impression that there are more extensions in play here than you'd find on Ronnie O'Sullivan's snooker cue, resulting in plenty of nooks and crannies to explore and ultimately relax in. Luckily for me I also found there was five well-kept real ales to choose from on the bar including three from Adnams Brewery, namely Southwold (3.7% bitter), Ghost Ship (4.5% pale ale) and Broadside (4.7% red ale) and two guests. Outside, to the rear, the Mariner prides itself on its well-designed terrace and decking with lawns that lead down to the sand dunes and the sea beyond; an idyllic setting for a beer and meal on a fine summer's evening as the sun sets over the Wash.

There was a sprinkling of Sunday lunch diners dotted around the pub but the main concentration of folk was a gathering from the local Royal National Lifeboat Institution (RNLI) who were all congregated within the immediate bar area. They were chatting away to each other in a carefree, bonhomie way and were in apparently good spirits. The adorable Alisha and I both thought that, considering the relaxed low-key manner, they'd just probably had a training session of some sort or maybe had just met up for a beer. But no! We found out the following day, in an article in the Eastern Daily Press by Charlotte Houldey, that the 'Spirit of West Norfolk' inshore lifeboat had been launched that Sunday morning at 10:57. A HM Coastguard spokesman said "HM Coastguard responded to an incident at Old Hunstanton this morning 21 May. At around 11am a Coastguard Rescue Team from Hunstanton and inshore lifeboat from Hunstanton RNLI were sent to the sea to assist." A man was pulled from the water and taken to hospital by the East of England Ambulance service. Fire crews and the police had also been at the scene.

It turns out they'd saved a life and were just celebrating a job done well with a nice pint and a natter. I doff my cap to these people...

It was deemed a positive that we'd made the effort to detour to Old Hunstanton as, once we'd made the short journey back into Hunstanton, we found the Wash and Tope disappointingly had just the one pricey cask ale on sale - Timothy Taylor's Landlord (4.3% bitter). As we queued to check-in a barman asked if anyone would like a drink while they were waiting. It was a 'No' from Neil and everyone else for that matter apart from a brick-shithouse of a fellow immediately to my right who said "Orate pal. I'll have a Landlord." There was no 'please', no 'thank you' thus confirming my suspicions that he was from West Yorkshire – I'm plumping for Bradford or 'Bratfut' as they say locally. The barman placed the pint on the bar and nonchalantly said "That'll be five pounds and seventy-five pence please." There was a huge intake of air from within the pub as the customer (who was from Yorkshire let's not forget, allegedly where the residents have the deepest pockets and shortest arms of all) maniacally looked back at the now trembling barman. "FIVE POUND...AND SEVENTY-FIVE PENCE...FURRA PINTA FUCKIN LANDLORD??? THIS'D BERRA BE...THE BEST PINT OF LANDLORD...EVVA" combusted the Yorkie, sort of kissing his teeth every so often in order to get rid of some imaginary apple skin. As he began to take a sip from a pint pot, that looked like a half in his massive hand, the pianist stopped playing, the couple of sluggers stopped brawling in the corner, the saloon gates silently flapped open and shut as the card school looked up from their table (ok I've made this last bit up but I swear the Sky Sports commentary of the West Ham/Leeds fixture did appear to go silent for a moment). He slowly and painstakingly placed the glass down on the bar as the whole pub waited with bated breath for the verdict. "Aye. It's orate is that. Bit pricey mind, but orate. Cheers." and commenced chatting to his partner.

There was something not quite right with the Wash and Tope and yet I couldn't rationally put my finger on why. Named after the nearby expanse of water and a breed of fish that can be found within, it had previously been called the Railway Hotel. Renamed in 1967 after the closure of the town's adjacent railway station (the cleared land now predictably functioning as a municipal car park) this family-owned establishment was extensively refurbished a few years ago. It serves traditional pub food, there's a pool table, it features a variety of sports on the TV's, has live music at the weekends and provides bed and breakfast accommodation with several rooms having attractive sea views. Basically it's covering most bases and yet it all appeared to be rather miserable for some inexplicable reason, as though there was a large dank and dark cloud enveloping it.

I'd initially spotted the place earlier that afternoon as the Coastliner bus had swung around the corner into Hunstanton, the pub frontage catching my eye as it's painted in the dullest grey colour imaginable. If there had been a competition to make the building look as gloomy as possible then the winner's plaque would have been presented with haste. Admittedly, once inside, the main bar area is comfortable and relatively bright but once through the door to the stiflingly narrow staircase that leads up to the rooms an air of melancholy prevailed. I'm no psychic, or psychometrist for that matter, but when I brushed the wall or held the door handle to our room I had an unsettling, almost eerie feeling that many, many people had been here before me. Without alarming Alisha I also began to ruminate if there could have been a macabre incident in the dim and distant past. And if so, could the memory of it still be troubling the building, hanging in the air, clinging to the wallpaper?

Early the following morning we agreed to skip the in-house breakfast offering although, on passing the dining room, I was heartened to recognise one familiar voice opining "It's orate is this breakfast. Bit pricey mind, but orate." On leaving the premises Leesh turned to me and said "I didn't want to say anything last night Dad but I'm pleased to be out of there to be honest. I don't know what it was but that place gave me the creeps."

There'll be more on the Wash and Tope later but, for now, it was time to begin our ramble along those 84 miles of the Norfolk Coast Path.

HUNSTANTON TO BURNHAM DEEPDALE

As the adorable Alisha and I stood close to the Hunstanton war memorial, there was no pomp and circumstance associated with the official starting point of this coastal walk along the eastern extremity of the UK; no brass bands playing or 21-gun salutes to enthuse us to get on our way. Handily nearby, there was a formal wooden waymarker on which 'Norfolk Coast Path' received top billing, just edging out 'St Edmund's Chapel' into second spot with 'Putting Green & Crazy Golf' receiving the wooden spoon.

Walking through this evidently popular and upbeat seaside town that Monday morning I'd been impressed. There was a sprinkling of early-bird couples sauntering along in that instantly recognisable holiday-mode fashion (you know, where they are holding hands but have already started arguing about where to go for breakfast) and most buildings appeared to be in a good state of repair. I'd also noticed several fish & chip shops (always a bonus), plus the gardens and greens looked to be well maintained. One of the latter was overseen by a life-size bronze statue of the generous local benefactor and splendidly named visionary Henry L'Estrange Styleman Le Strange, proudly looking out over a resort that he had played a fundamental role in creating during the mid-1800's.

The Le Strange's family pile was Hunstanton Hall and Victorian nobleman Henry was determined to see the area developed into a successful seaside town to rival others that he knew to be thriving further down the British coastline, at Brighton and Southend. His imagination and passion for the project convinced investors to back his idea while also crucially providing the funding for a railway line to transport prospective visitors there. Dying suddenly in 1862 from heart disease he was never to see his grand plan completely come to fruition. There is no doubt that without him Hunstanton would not be the admired location it is today, attracting thousands of holidaymakers every summer. The statue is a fitting and enduring tribute to a man whose vision created what we see there nowadays.

Those early Victorian trippers would no doubt have been impressed when they first set sight on the town's distinctively striped and coloured cliffs. The stripes, consisting of different coloured rocks (white chalk, red limestone and brown carstone), were laid down at the bottom of oceans between 93 and 112 million years ago. With the global climate then being much warmer and sea levels a lot higher than they are currently, this area was a lot closer to the equator and enjoyed a similar climate to that presently experienced in the Bahamas. It's hard to take in, isn't it? I'm sure that I'm not the only one who's struggled to grasp that this area was once to be found at the bottom of a warm tropical sea. The 18-metre-high cliffs are officially classed as being exceptional, deemed a Site of Special Scientific Interest for their geology.

We were not destined to see the cliffs for ourselves – the tide was in. For us it was a steady and inconspicuous start along the cliff tops. However, we hadn't walked very far at all before our first real photo opportunity of the trip cropped up. Firstly, we came across the remains of St Edmund's Chapel (erected in 1272) that included an attractive archway; behind the archway was the suitably situated Hunstanton lighthouse, now being utilised as a quirky guesthouse. We immediately started enjoying ourselves just a little too much, almost giddy-like. "Take one of me Leesh in the archway…make sure you get the lighthouse in though! Hahaha!", "Take one of me Dad…you sure you've got the lighthouse in? Hahaha!" Oh what fun we were having. Five minutes into an 84 mile walk and it's an absolute doddle. Nice weather, plenty of energy, clearly marked coast path and a super sure-footed surface. It's an absolute cinch this walking malarkey (and, yep, I'd already taken my eye off the ball with as much aplomb as an Ipswich Town centre half defending a corner).

What is worth mentioning at this stage is that it is crucial to have a really good guidebook to refer to along the journey and I had plumped for Phoebe Smith's 'Walking the Peddars Way and Norfolk Coast Path'. I'd had a look at a few others (which were also very good and extremely informative) but it was Phoebe's that won the day for me. I considered the detail to be clear and concise, it contained maps that were easy to follow and the pocket size of the publication meant it was easy to handle; perfect then for the novice long distance walker such as myself. In the weeks leading up to our hike I'd read the guide numerous times in the hope that key information would sink in. Once on the walk, of course, all you must do is continue to read the relevant pages and consult it at key moments.

A couple of kilometres further along the path, from

St Edmund's chapel and the lighthouse, we were lost. I say 'we' when it was me alone who'd taken us along the incorrect route. I was the chief fuckwit. But please let me explain...

Anyone who lives in Norfolk or is a regular visitor there will be eager to tell you about the vast open spaces that are to be found. The west of the county (as we have already ascertained) is part of the Fens, the centre is gently undulating lowlands, in the east are a network of rivers and lakes known as the Broads while the north and east look out over the North Sea. You can go birdwatching, boating, running, cycling and explore the vast swathes of beaches at your own leisure. Norfolk is choc-o-bloc full of space, if you know what I mean.

Yet, less than an hour after cracking on from that first waymarker, I was boxed in by wooden beach-huts that were nestled into the dunes a few yards to my left. Between them, Alisha and I were waist-high in coarse grass with the same immediately to our right. The 'clearly marked and super sure-footed surface' at the outset was no longer straightforward, now just a mere parting on the sandy floor created by someone who had travelled the same way in the last couple of days. It wasn't a well-trodden path. Completing the scene was a chain link fence just a metre over to the right. It all felt overly restricting.

"This can't be right Leesh" I complained. "We must have gone wrong somewhere. Let me have a look up these dunes and see what's beyond them." I carried on, wafting my guidebook in the air towards the general direction of what could have been Leverton Highgate, Wrangle Bank or even maybe Friskney Flats for that matter, over in Lincolnshire. To my unbridled joy there was a decent-looking path leading down towards the sea and flanking off in the general direction that we needed to be going. "Here we are! This is where we need to be" I exclaimed with as much glee as someone who'd been lost on a desert island for a month. "Come on, we're back on track."

A quick look at Phoebe's guide would have simply advised me to '*Follow the path along here, long grass tracing it either side, until it returns you to the corner of the fenceline with the golf course. Here the path curves round to the right. Follow it, ignoring the path that leads down to the sea*'. But, with the book faithfully contained within my right hand, I didn't even give it a glance.

I then proceeded to take us on the wildest of goose chases for a good half an hour. The further we went without coming across the sandy crossroads at Holme next the Sea, where the Peddars Way meets the coast path, the more I was obtaining that nagging and sinking feeling. 'Shall we turn around?', 'I think we need to go back' and 'I've definitely messed up here' all came into my mind before the decision was finally made for us. A purposefully placed fence abruptly blocked our path but beyond this was an uncrossable and very large pond. It was either swim through it (never an option, honestly) or retrace our steps for another unnecessary 30 minutes. To make matters worse, the previous day I'd been preaching to Alisha the benefits of strictly keeping to the route to protect our legs and not having to do any extra mileage. It was the first part of day one and I'd single handedly taken us at least an hour out of our way.

"What's that what you're singing Leeshy?" I enquired, as we retraced our steps towards the elusive Holme. "Lost by Frank Ocean" she replied, emanating a little chuckle.

It felt good to be finally back on track and, after passing Holme Bird Observatory and Nature Reserve, it wasn't too long before an iconic (and much photographed and painted) coal barn loomed into view on the edge of the mud flats. I was very happy to clap eyes on this building as I realised we were close to the village of Thornham where we would be undertaking our first 'refreshment' stop of the day. Considering that the 2011 census documented that there was just under 500 inhabitants residing here I found it somewhat impressive that there were three public houses (Lifeboat, Chequers and Orange Tree) to entice us through their doors and I made a dash for the first one we saw which was the Orange Tree…or was it the King's Head? My confusion arose due to there being two conflicting pubs signs outside. The distinctive one (and looking a lot more established) was an elaborate and very intricate metal outer-design with a portrait of a king's head contained within. This was proudly hanging from a traditional wooden support that we are accustomed to seeing on the edge of pub car parks all over the country. Situated underneath was the more contemporary 'Orange Tree' sign, the type of which you'd expect to find popping up outside a 'soon to be opening' health club.

Once inside, all was explained by the lady who served me an excellent pint of Moongazer Cheeky Jack, a 5% IPA and the 2023 champion beer of Norfolk. Woodforde's Wherry (3.8% amber ale) and Lacons Vista (4.2% pale ale) were the other two ales on sale. She informed me that the striking King's Head sign had been made locally at Thornham Wrought Iron Works (founded 1887 and closed 1916) over 100 years ago and had become listed, along with the building, in 1953. The renaming to the Orange Tree had occurred after a change of ownership in October 2005.

Suitably refreshed, it was now time to re-commence our hike along the Norfolk COAST Path. You know the one; it's where you may think you'd get to walk along the COAST of Norfolk...apart from the not so trivial matter of there being no suitable COASTAL access between Thornham and Brancaster. There is, of course, the A149 that separates the two villages. However, it would not be good for your safety and health to venture any further than two feet down this unofficial racetrack where idiotic drivers of high-performance vehicles (insert make/model here) appear to relish constant testosterone-fuelled 'Coastal Road' skirmishes with any other fellow lunatic who fancies taking up the challenge (and there are plenty). For the next couple of hours therefore, it would have to be the most tedious of walks for us, around three sides of a square, initially leaving the COAST behind as we headed off inland in a south-easterly direction.

Wished-for picturesque sea views and refreshing salty-aired breezes that stimulated the senses were exchanged for the plumbline straight Choseley Road (that was in the process of being re-laid with malodorous tarmac), a dull copse, dusty dirt tracks and stretches along the edge of farmer's fields where, once again, we had to wade through waist-high grass. My thighs and Achilles tendons were already beginning to ache at this stage (probably related to the extra mileage accrued around the Holme next the Sea area) and it was a relief, as we descended past some picturesque cottages, to reach Brancaster. I glanced over to my right, checking for the wannabee Lewis Hamilton's along the A149, and gleefully spotted the Ship Hotel. Optimistically looking over at Alisha, she forthrightly instructed "Don't even think about it big lad. We've got another mile and a half to get in yet before our day is finished and we need to keep going." Bugger.

Up until November 2022, if we had wanted to reach our final destination for the day at Burnham Deepdale, we would have traversed along a 1.7km wooden boardwalk, raised above extremely boggy reed beds. This route had now been closed due to its rapid deterioration making it unsafe. The good news was that funding (reported to be a cool £1,060,000) had been obtained with work subsequently planned for later in the year and beyond, to repair the damaged surface with a longer-lasting glass reinforced plastic (GRP) substance – it was expected that the new boardwalk would remain in good condition for the next 80 years. Aggregate paths at the beginning and end of the boardwalk would also be installed.

A clearly signposted alternative route was in place that guided us along sleepy back lanes and tranquil cottages before dumping us abruptly back on 'that' main road, which along this stretch was unsurprisingly and unimaginatively called 'Main Road' (there's obvious justification to 'jazz up' the road name to something like Circuito Brancazza, Kartodromo Brancasto or even Brancaster Raceway). I knew we were close to the day's initial finishing line and after a short while there it was - the Jolly Sailors public house.

An award-winning pub that welcomes 'families, muddy or sandy boots and muddy paws', this 18th century village local is the focal point for their very own five-barrel Brancaster Brewery. Independent and family-owned, it continues an apparently long, illustrious tradition of beer production in the area with evidence of brewing going back as early as Roman times. The pub also boasts the largest selection of rum on the Norfolk coast, plus there's an excellent menu covering local seafood, stone baked pizzas and great pub classics.

Dusty, sweaty and with burning hamstrings that now appeared to be comfortingly swathed in imaginary hot water bottles, I plonked myself down in the snug as Leesh brought me over a pint of Brancaster Oyster Catcher, a 4.4% golden ale that was both refreshing and moreish (Woodforde's Wherry was also available). The blurb says that the beer is 'best drunk watching the sun go down over the marshes at Brancaster Staithe' and it may well be for most people. But on that particular Monday afternoon, I can quite happily confess that my preference was to sup it in that unpretentious and pleasantly rustic pub, relaxingly viewing the posters on the wall featuring pictures of North Norfolk tourist hotspots that included Holkham Beach, Cley Windmill and Creake Abbey. Content with our exertions, it was lovely to reflect on a pleasurable day of walking, a job well done.

Food-wise I plumped for the hefty ½lb beef & bone marrow burger that came with lettuce, coleslaw, tomato and fries. I also ordered an extra portion of fries as yes, I am a greedy sod but my aching body was seriously craving the carbs. "Don't drop that on your foot mate or you'll break your toes" observed a concerned chap (John from Leicester) on the next table as I was about to take my first bite. Curiously, his face portrayed the knowing look of someone who had, on such an occasion, dropped a ½lb beef & bone marrow burger on his foot and actually broke his toes although (call me perceptive) I suspect that this had probably not been the case. Alisha had the whole tail scampi, chips, peas and tartare sauce. Absolutely delightful.

Our mini pub tour for the day was not quite over yet as half a mile away, on the opposite side of the road, can be found the Jolly Sailors sister pub, the White Horse. There is more to this venue than the dispensing of drinks. Classy ensuite rooms are available to be booked plus the ever-popular restaurant at the rear of the place overlooks the Brancaster Bay tidal marsh. From here you can wrap yourself up in the stunning and atmospheric views towards Scolt Head Island and the sea beyond. A nice touch is that local fish and shellfish is obtained from fishermen whose oyster and mussel beds are situated at the bottom of the garden.

Oysters??? Oysters??? Did somebody mention oysters???

"Excuse me. I'd like to point out that I do have a crustacean allergy but I'd still like to order a dozen oysters please" said a cheery lady over to our left as we waited to get served at the bar.

"You've got to be fucking kidding me" answered the slightly flustered waitress. Not really, that was what I was thinking. She actually informed the requester that 'the kitchen' would have to make the decision whether to serve them or not. When she returned the answer was negative – no molluscs would be served. The now not-so-cheery customer got up, stamped her feet a little, while complaining "the decision should be mine if I'm willing to take the risk" and promptly left.

It reminded me of my trips to Doncaster to see my sister. We usually pop into a pub near the railway station and when we order food the lady taking the order always asks "Have you got any allergies todaaaaaaaayyy?" It's almost as though she's expecting me to say "Well, I must admit that yesterday I had a nut allergy but today I'm sure I'll be fine. So, for table 14, I'll have chicken and cashew nuts please, thank you very much. If I come in tomorrow, I do appreciate that I could be lactose intolerant for 24 hours. Cheers."

For the record, four cask beers were on the bar in the White Horse: Brancaster Oyster Catcher, Greene King Abbot Ale (5% extra special bitter), Woodforde's Wherry and Barsham Golden Close (5% 'Norfolk IPA'). I chose the latter as my final pint of the day (OK, I may have had a couple) and very nice they were too.

A combination of an early start to the day, the miles hiked, the large meal recently consumed and the drink imbibed had all contributed to me starting to feel a bit sleepy. Also, the background music being played on the pub's sound system didn't help – it was the dreamy blend of moody non-descriptive tunes you'd find in an aquarium - and so, rather than risk falling asleep on my stool unglamorously slobbering all over the bar towels, I decided to 'draw stumps' for the day and headed for our accommodation at Deepdale Camping & Rooms. I do not exaggerate when I say this is an absolute gem of a place.

An eco-friendly campsite with private rooms, it is situated on the organic Deepdale Farm. The following are all welcome on the site: tents, trailer tents, campervans, motorhomes, recreational vehicles, hammocks and winnebagos (the latter being 'a motor vehicle with living accommodation used when travelling long distances or camping' and not to be confused with 'a member of a North American people formerly living in eastern Wisconsin and now mainly in southern Wisconsin and Nebraska' although I'm sure they'd be more than welcome too. Phew, I'm please we've cleared that up). I found it intriguing that caravans are not allowed but this is apparently due to planning restrictions.

The Stables and The Granary areas offer comfortable self-catering private rooms with both en suite and shared facilities. I'd booked a twin room with single beds for the princely sum of £56.70 that included a handy 10% 'green' deduction for walking there and not using a vehicle. In an area where £180 is the norm for a one-night stay (if you can get a one-night stay that is, as most places only offer a minimum of two nights) this place is an absolute diamond in the rough.

Also enjoying well-drained pitches, electric hookups and underfloor heated shower blocks, Deepdale has recently received the well-deserved accolade of AA Small Campsite of the Year.

There is a strict 'no noise' policy after 10pm to

ensure that everyone can enjoy a relaxed and peaceful sleep. On a purely personal note, I can confirm that if a herd of large-hoofed buffaloes with imposing horns on their heads had come snorting and stampeding through the site during the night (OK, I concede that this is a highly unlikely event in North Norfolk) I am sure that I would not have stirred one iota.

But…before I turned the light out I still had one insistent question going around in my mind that I needed to find an answer for before I could rest completely for the night, and that was: What had occurred in the past at the Wash and Tope in Hunstanton that could possibly have been directly responsible for the melancholy that I felt enshrouded the building? I hadn't been searching online for very long before I stumbled across the following newspaper report, attributed to the Sheffield Evening Telegraph and dated 'Sat 4 January 1902'.

'SHOCKING HOTEL TRAGEDY

-PROPRIETOR SHOT

-ASSISTANT MANAGER'S SUICIDE'

A shocking tragedy occurred at the Railway Hotel, Hunstanton, on Thursday night when the proprietor, Mr. Edward Wales, was shot by Hubert Klee, the assistant manager, who then committed suicide. Mr. Wales is in a serious condition, but he is expected to recover.

Both were young men (under 28 years of age), and until

the last few months had been on good terms. Klee originally came to Hunstanton as a pianist on the pier, and he and Mr. Wales became great friends. The Railway Hotel was at that time conducted by the mother of Mr. Wales, but the lady retired at the end of last season and her son then made Klee the assistant manager.

Recently the two men had been on bad terms. Klee had told several people that he would shoot Wales. When Mr. Wales returned home on Thursday night, the housekeeper warned him of Klee's threats. However, Wales took off his coat and went into the bar. The housekeeper got between the two men, but Klee, pointing a revolver at Wales, said, "If you value your life, go away." Then turning round to a customer in the bar, he said, "If you don't go, I will shoot you." The customer hurried out. Meantime Wales had pushed away the housekeeper. Klee then, turning round, said, "One for you," and shot Wales over the eye, inflicting a severe wound. He then put the pistol to his own head, and saying, "One for me," fired two shots and died at once.'

According to the Norfolk Pubs website (who have the proprietor listed as Ernest Wales) Hubert Klee's funeral took place on Sunday 5th January and several hundred people attended. The congregation were informed that he had been 'punctilious in his religious duties but had fallen away of late, drawn away by a life which was eminently unfitted to the temperament of the poor lad, whose sad end had spread such gloom over their small community'.

By mid-June 1902, Ernest Wales had put the whole contents of the hotel up for auction, relinquishing all ties with the business as a consequence of ongoing ill-health issues as a result of the shooting.

Day 1 miles walked: 15.92 / Total miles walked: 15.92

BURNHAM DEEPDALE
TO STIFFKEY

I slept like a log for 10 blissful hours and after a rejuvenating shower felt like a million dollars, wholly enthused for the exertions and experiences that lay ahead. The air of trepidation that had enveloped me in the lead up to the walk had dissipated long ago. The pre-walk butterflies in my stomach had fluttered away into the atmosphere followed by the aches and pains that had afflicted my muscles and joints just the previous evening.

My daughter and I had timed our room departure to synchronise with that of the opening of Deepdale Café next door where a full English belly-buster was within our sights. However, on arrival we were greeted by a hand-written notice sellotaped to the window advising 'Kitchen closed. No food today'.

Now normally, in a village as relatively remote as Burnham Deepdale is, this would be an issue as the breakfast alternatives would be as thin on the ground as, well, breakfast alternatives in a remote village. This was not a problem here as the café is part of the splendid Dalegate Market, an independent retail venue that contains outlets selling clothes and accessories, souvenirs and jewellery. It is home to a Visitor Information Centre, there's a 'nature shop' (where you can purchase wildlife-watching kit such as binoculars and telescopes), a glass studio, a gallery that includes a pottery, a place to hire bikes and there's also a fuel station. It's a major hub on this part of the coast, offering a place to shop, eat, drink and generally mooch around for a couple of hours, if that's your thing.

Crucially, and more pertinently for us at half past seven in the morning, there was also a well-stocked supermarket that had already opened its doors for the day. I selected a rhubarb compote, yoghurt and granola combo pot accompanied by, wait for it, two jumbo sausage rolls. I know, I know - an absolutely inspired choice (stick with me for more tips of gastronomic delight). The breakfast of champions indeed.

As we headed away from Burnham Deepdale and back onto the official path the sun started to break through for what was promising to be another glorious day in May; just chilly enough to wear a lightweight 'weather' jacket but equally pleasant enough for the walk to be enjoyed. There was no rain and a gentle, refreshing wind to help us on our way.

The raised seabank, that we were now pacing along, was sufficiently elevated to provide us with simply spectacular views over the uniquely bleak and yet utterly beautiful vista over towards the silvery sea far away on the horizon. Twisting, muddy tidal creeks, treacherous to cross and yet so pleasurable to view, contained discarded boats with some looking like they had been there for a very long time. This all added to the overall feeling of wonderful isolation. A rich and colourful array of plant life provided the perfect haven for an abundance of raucous migratory birds (it would have been nice at this stage to distinguish my Knots from my Godwits, my Dunlins from my Shelducks but it wasn't to be). This is the view that the lucky patrons from the White Horse look out onto from the drinking and eating areas at the rear of the establishment.

It was at this point that I 'rolled' my ankle and immediately thought 'I hope that doesn't come back to bite me'. Well actually, my initial thought was 'Fuck, that hurt' but I suppose you'd have guessed that anyway. I could see that the path had recently been extremely muddy but this had now dried to leave a hard and rutted surface with narrow furrows, almost as though a heavy tricycle operated by an equally heavy person had travelled along this part of the route while sodden. I'd previously been carefully walking along, vigilantly watching my feet placement, making sure I stopped before taking in the views but on this sole occasion I made the schoolboy error – if ever there was one – of carrying on instead of stopping to make my observations. After a slight pause I gingerly re-commenced my journey. "Are you alright there big lad?" queried an observant Alisha.

"All good here duck" I answered. Well, all good for the present anyway...

After sweeping around the marshes of Burnham Deepdale and Burnham Norton we crossed the River Burn, skirted along the edge of another kindly farmer's field and arrived in the small hamlet of Burnham Overy Staithe. Now, the eagle-eyed amongst you will have detected that there is quite a lot of 'Burnham-ing' going on in this north-westerly part of Norfolk. This is all to do with the aforementioned waterway (locally known as Nelson's River) that flows through the area for seven and a half miles from its source, one mile south of the village of South Creake, to its mouth at Overy Creek.

The original Norfolk Burnhams was a group of seven adjacent villages 'by the sea', all within a radius of two miles, with a few warranting a mention in the Domesday Book of 1086. These were: Burnham Norton, Burnham Overy, Burnham Thorpe, Burnham Deepdale, Burnham Westgate, Burnham Ulph and Burnham Sutton. They even warranted their own mnemonic which was *'Nelson Of Thorpe Died Well Under Sail'*.

There is a common conception that Burnham Market was one of the original seven but this is incorrect. It is a modern merging of the Burnham's Sutton, Westgate and Ulph, these three central villages forming a larger one that is now a civil parish and principal centre for the Burnhams as well as several other nearby villages. Relatively recently, Burnham Market has acquired the nickname of Chelsea on Sea due to the considerable number of Londoners who have purchased a second home there.

The eagle, eagle-eyed of you will no doubt have spotted that Admiral Lord Horatio Nelson is also beginning to get a mention in these annals. Viewed by many as 'Norfolk's favourite son' he was extremely proud of his roots, once famously addressing a crowd outside the Wrestlers Inn in Great Yarmouth (after his return from the Battle of the Nile) with the iconic statement *'I am myself a Norfolk man and glory in being so'*.

Born in Burnham Thorpe he is believed to have

learnt to row and sail a dinghy in the staithe (meaning a landing stage for boats and derived from the old Norse word stoth) at Burnham Overy at the age of ten before joining the navy two years later. The rest, as they say, is (ahem) history. A hero for many sailors past and present he was renowned for his leadership, seamanship and courage in battles in which he tended to be rather successful. He's celebrated not only in his native county but also further afield such as in the nation's capital where he's the focal point in Trafalgar Square looking out from his very own impressive column. Other monuments, created in his honour, stand elsewhere in the world such as in Place Jacques-Cartier, Montreal, Canada. This also happens to be that city's oldest remaining monument.

Furthermore, if you happen to be travelling by road into this easterly shire, the respective road signs also pay homage by informing motorists in no uncertain terms that they are entering 'NORFOLK Nelson's County'.

Believe it or not, there's also a tribute on the outskirts of Chesterfield, on top of the rocky Birchen Edge that overlooks Baslow in the Derwent Valley. This monument consists of a three-metre-tall gritstone obelisk with a thirty-centimetre ball balanced on top. It was erected in 1810 by a suitably impressed local businessman called John Brightman. Behind the monument lay the 'Three Ships', large outcrops also of gritstone that are carved with the names of three of Nelson's vessels at the Battle of Trafalgar, namely Victory, Defiance and Royal Soverin (sic).

The 'Visit Norfolk' website has the Admiral down as being a bit of a card. Here are three examples (and bear in mind he had just the one arm, plus one of his eyes could only differentiate between light and dark):

1. At a swearing-in ceremony (where he was to receive the Freedom of the Borough of Great Yarmouth) he placed his left hand on the bible. The clerk said "Your right hand, my lord" to which Nelson replied "*That* is in Tenerife."

2. During the Battle of Copenhagen his men were under heavy bombardment. He refused orders to withdraw, raising his telescope to his 'dead' eye and commenting "I really do not see the signal."

3. When Admiral Nelson was alive he was 5 feet tall. He now has a statue that is 25 feet tall. That's Horatio of 5:1.

OK, I may have made the last one up.

Burnham Overy Staithe has a public house that dates to the middle of the nineteenth century. Now you are aware of Nelson's standing in this area it will not surprise you to learn that the hostelry is called the Hero. Also of no surprise will be that the pub sign, more often than not over the years, has incorporated a painting of the Admiral. Yet the Norfolk Pubs website reports that in 1963 this was controversially replaced by pub owners (and Norwich brewers) Steward and Patteson Ltd to that of Wing Commander Guy Gibson VC (a distinguished and much-decorated bomber pilot of Dambusters fame). This caused such an uproar in the hamlet that the original sign was re-hung within a week.

Even though the pub officially opens its doors for trade mid-morning we were still too early to pay a visit. Instead, we sauntered down to the staithe. Here we were delightfully greeted by three people (two in wet suits, one in a bikini – all glorious in pink bathing caps) who were on their way into the water for a, no doubt, exhilarating pre-lunch swim. The sun was shining, the boats were bobbing about on the twinkling surface; the lovely setting reminiscent of one that used to be found on a picture postcard. We sat down to enjoy this view, the adorable Alisha sensibly hydrating with a bottle of water, me re-fuelling with my second and final jumbo sausage roll.

We waved goodbye to the swimmers while also bidding farewell to the cheery proprietors of the ferry, that takes explorers to the nearby Scolt Head Island nature reserve, who were patiently waiting for their first customers of the day. There was still a challenging ten miles to hike before reaching our destination for this second day at Stiffkey.

The next section of the walk, leading to the bustling little town of Wells-next-the- Sea, promised to be a very stimulating one as it incorporated a contrast of terrains and sights including the taxing Gun Hill dunes, the vast expanse of Holkham Beach and an enchanting path through a forest that eventually culminated in the long, long walk along a raised causeway, a sea defence locally referred to as 'The Bank', into Wells.

I particularly enjoyed reaching the beach at Holkham. After a good 24 hours of seemingly being nowhere near the sea, with only the occasional tantalising far-away glimpse, it was reassuring to have it once more accompanying us on our left-hand side. There's miles and miles of soft white sand here on what is surely one of the widest expanses and most spectacular of UK beaches. The softness of the sand did make for heavy going so we attempted to find a more convenient route by walking nearer to the tide that was on its way out - this was not to be beneficial though as we found the surface to be 'gloopy', thereby utilising our own private dialect. Soft, dry sand it was then for the next couple of miles. This would certainly be a test for my ankle before reaching the firmer footing of the wooden boardwalk at Holkham Gap…

Wells came into view, touristy with plenty of moored-up boats resting in the harbour. There was an evident hustle and bustle to the town that we had not encountered since Hunstanton; amusement arcades, fish and chip shops, ice-cream parlours, souvenir emporiums and all the other seasidey things that are popular with throngs of day-trippers. We carried on around the waterfront and under the overhang of the old granary before walking through a boatyard. Here, the general hub-hub and chitter-chatter of the town had quickly been replaced by what appeared to be the constant sound of bicycle bells being rung by a group of deranged cyclists on steroids. I was unsure whether the weird sound was being made by the shrouds slapping against the metal masts or if special wind operated bells had been fitted onto the boats to deter pesky seagulls from causing any damage. As I could not see any of the feathered intruders, either ploy must have been working.

Those atmospheric saltmarshes began to dominate the landscape once more, accompanied by the extensive, wide-open spaces and captivating Norfolk sky, with the sea appearing every now and again over the horizon. Easy walking along an embankment changed abruptly into an undulating, narrow trail that initially headed through a copse before emerging into a mixture of long grass, nettles and weeds. My imagination ran wild as I visualised this part of the path having been a busy, primeval route where traders once transported their goods (obtained through fair means such as farming or foul such as smuggling) to buyers located along these ancient villages and hamlets. There was an overwhelming feeling of remoteness where we had not seen a soul for ages and then, to our complete surprise, we walked around a blind corner to find an elderly couple relaxing on a neatly laid-out chequered blanket, a laden wicker picnic basket in front of them, taking in the spectacular views. "Good afternoon" they said. "Good afternoon" we replied. There was no need to say anymore.

We eventually arrived in the charming, sleepy little village of Stiffkey after heading up Green Way from the coast path. Only a couple of hundred people live here and yet it is rich with tales of notable ex-residents and folklore plus it has its very own type of shellfish known as 'Stewkey Blues'. Let me start by telling you about the latter…

Stiffkey (or Stewkey) Blues are cockles with a blue hue that are best collected from sand beds located in an area called Blacknock which is situated between the creeks of High Sand and Stone Mell that lay outside the village. They obtain their distinctive blue colouring from the mud and sand in which they live. Reputedly the best cockles you'll ever taste, I am led to believe that this local delicacy (revered by chefs across England) is best served with lashings of vinegar and a healthy sprinkling of black pepper. Arguably, they were Stiffkey's main claim to fame until 1906 when one Harold Francis Davidson became the Rector of Stiffkey and Morston.

Born in 1875 he was educated at Oxford and is believed to have earned his own university fees through his success as a comedic actor (I've seen quite a lot of photographs of the Rector and the likeness of him to that of the hugely successful comic actor Alastair Sim in the wacky, side-splitting 1954 film The Belles of St. Trinian's is truly uncanny – this is where Sim plays the dual role of headmistress Miss Millicent Fritton and her twin brother Clarence Fritton). All was ticking along nicely for him before he experienced an epiphany while saving a teenage girl who was in the act of throwing herself into the River Thames. Ever since that event he had an insatiable appetite for helping 'that type of girl' who may have been stranded and also needed help on the alluring and yet mean streets of London.

Hyperactive and totally unconventional, he was

unsuited (uncomfortable even) to the role of being priest in a remote north Norfolk parish. He quickly began leading a double life, where the draw of London's Soho, where he ministered to a rather different flock, enthused him to catch the first train there on a Monday morning from Wells-next-the-Sea. He would not return until the last train on a Saturday night.

His alternative and unofficial parishioners for much of the week were considered by many in church circles to be down and outs and prostitutes (he styled himself on being the 'Prostitutes Padre'). In reality, he was assisting girls of a certain age who had fallen on hard times, encouraging as many as he could to improve their circumstances, although it is known that he did have a priority for aiding the ones who had 'good white teeth'. What is not clear, and I guess we shall never know now, is if the fine line between helping/saving the young girls and adoring them became blurred at some stage as time wore on.

Meanwhile, his official parishioners rightly began to feel neglected and it's fair to say that he didn't help himself on occasions. He would often turn up to church on a Sunday morning in a dishevelled state, once being so late for communion that he rode his bicycle straight down the aisle before propping it up against the altar. This all lead to unsubstantiated rumours among locals that he had been engaging in extra-curricular activities in the nearby sand dunes with his young girl friends, some of whom he would bring back to Norfolk to meet his wife and five children.

He carried on for years with this chaotic and unconventional commuting life with seemingly very little official objection to it (although the church was aware and was concerned), that is, until one fateful day when he undiplomatically demanded that a dominant parishioner, Major Philip Hamond, must buy the land around the grave of his first wife if he sought to look after it. The major complained to the Bishop of Norwich thus setting in motion an investigation, with the Rector now finding himself positioned at the top of a very slippery slope.

First of all, Miss Rose Ellis (who he'd known since 1920, at one time having paid for her treatment for syphilis), spilt the beans to a private detective hired indirectly by the bishop, stating that she'd had a relationship with Davidson. Interestingly, the detective had interviewed nearly fifty girls and yet this had been the only statement complaining about the Rector's behaviour. The snag here was that she admitted a week later that the detective had plied her with port and lemon in order to loosen her tongue. She recanted her story, sorry and ashamed.

Unfortunately, by this time Davidson had sold his own version of the story to the Empire News, seeing the situation as an excellent opportunity to preach about love and of his 'ministry' to the fallen girls of Soho. He became exultant, writing more articles, preaching more sermons and became very famous in doing so. Nevertheless, even though there was no concrete evidence of guilt, he was charged with five counts of immoral behaviour, one which included embracing a girl in a Chinese restaurant. What probably sank him in the end was a photograph of him with a 15-year-old girl called Estelle Douglas, who just happened to be naked. It later transpired that this photo had been staged by the same detective who had sought to bribe Rose Ellis.

The trial opened on March 29th 1932 and attracted a great deal of public attention - a cause célèbre indeed. Sleepy Stiffkey was now as notorious as Babylon with Davidson as renowned as Al Capone and the village packed with people every weekend. Lasting for 25 days, the Chancellor left to work on his summing up on the 6th June before later finding the Rector guilty on all five charges. He was given a fortnight's notice to leave the church, effectively being removed, deposed and degraded all-in-one and this is where the story becomes even more peculiar.

Davidson decided to mimic the Greek philosopher

Diogenes who had sat in a tub believing one should be free from shame, emotion and useless conventions. The Rector chose to sit in a barrel on Blackpool promenade for 14 hours a day, deliberately positioning himself between a fasting woman and a flea circus as part of a sideshow. Muttering 'desperate ills require desperate remedies' he was attempting to raise £2,000 to appeal against his convictions. He was soon fined for obstruction after upwards of 3,000 people had visited him.

As time passed he realised that less people were taking notice of him and less people were listening. His campaign to clear his name, that had been initially very real, became ever-more-gimmicky resulting in him deciding to 'lecture' from the shocking confines of a lion's cage at a Skegness amusement park. You know what comes next.

On arrival he thought there would only be one lion but as he reached the cage he found there were two, a male and a female. Unsurprisingly he questioned if this was safe or not (I think I may have been able to answer that question for him) before either courageously or foolishly he decided to go ahead with the stunt anyway, thus acting out the classical Christian martyrdom. After fighting wildly and gallantly he was killed in full view of a gawping mob of onlookers. The lion tamer, showing great bravery, managed to get his body away from the rabid animals and out of the cage in a futile attempt to save *him* – ironically, she was a sixteen-year-old girl called Irene.

An old newspaper article (telling the tale of Harold Davidson) by Ronald Blythe, titled 'NAUGHTIEST VICAR OF THEM ALL' proudly hangs on the wall in Stiffkey's only remaining pub, the Red Lion. At one stage there had been three major hostelries in the village, these included the Victoria that closed its doors for good in 1962 and the Townshend Arms, likewise in 1971. We can consider ourselves extremely fortunate to be able to visit the Red Lion in our time as this pub also ceased trading in 1965 and remained a private house for a further 26 years. A big 'Well Done' to Chris and Adrienne Cooke who purchased the property in 1989 and decided to change it back into a pub. You don't see that very often do you? Usually, once they've gone, they've gone. Interestingly, the same family still run the pub to this day. I'm not sure what it would have looked like back in the 1960's when it closed but you can imagine that the interior layout has possibly not been altered a great deal since, if at all. There are several characterful drinking and dining areas warmed by log fires while at the rear is a nicely maintained, covered patio area. On our visit there were three local beers on offer, these being Woodforde's Wherry, Adnams Ghost Ship and (one of my personal favourites) Woodforde's Nelson's Revenge which is a classic 4.5% bitter. Another big pat on the back for the owners from me for retaining the old-style Woodforde's pump clips that I consider to be more effective and appealing than the newer, insipid versions.

It was good to see the pub thriving with a refreshing mixture of punters. A few locals were sat around the bar who, although having a good old mardle among themselves while quaffing their Wherrys, had time for a cheery word with me when I kept going up to order. "Ee's back for anither one, look! He loves his Nelson's dewn't 'e? Must be parched doin' all that traipsin!" Most people had come in for a meal though including a couple of elegant ladies who sat on the next table to Alisha and I and were also very amiable, politely asking us about our walk and where we were from. When our food arrived (Pork Loin, sourced from nearby Walsingham Farm, thank you very much) they both commented on how nice it looked and both decided to order the same for themselves. All was convivial, all very lovely…that was apart from a bloke (shall we call him Knobhead? I think we should) who was sat in the corner with his, no doubt, long suffering partner.

Now I'm not suggesting for one minute that the service was super quick with food flying out of the kitchen every 5 minutes, after the microwave has dinged for attention, with the staff dementedly running around rapidly serving people. This is rural Norfolk after all and sometimes you've got to wait a little while. They'll get round to serving you when they're ready and when it's your turn. All is orderly and pleasant. The specially prepared food (proudly all local produce) listed on the small yet perfectly formed menu will be flawlessly cooked to order and then professionally served to you at your table. This is how it should be. This is why we visit such places after all – the much undervalued slower and gentler pace of life.

The conscientious waitress was quietly and efficiently going about her business, effortlessly gliding around the tables making sure she updated everyone with where they currently were in the Red Lion's very own food chain. This included her saying to 'Knobhead' "I'll be with you in five minutes to take your order" before she went up the small flight of steps into the kitchen.

He wasn't happy, raising his arms in the air, palms facing upwards. "This is taking the bladdy mickey. We've been here for ten bladdy minutes already and we've still got to wait another bladdy five before we can order. Bladdy pathetic. I'm not coming back here again tomorrow. I'll go to the local supermarket and give them our bladdy money instead." His wife never looked up from staring at her placemat. She'd heard it all before and now he was making sure we all heard it. The ladies on the adjacent table to us discreetly raised their eyebrows. I thought 'Good luck in finding a supermarket in Stiffkey, Knobhead'.

After the allotted five minutes the waitress returned to the table, her pen expectantly hovering over her notepad. "OK, what would you like to order please."

"Well," harrumphed Knobhead "before I order you'll have to bladdy explain the menu to me. It makes no bladdy sense."

"Oh…err Ok. What is it that you'd like explaining?" the concerned waitress asked.

Knobhead stabbed his podgy finger against the menu. "This here! What on earth is it???!!!!"

By this stage Knobhead had got everyone's attention in the pub, which is probably what he was after in the first place. We all waited expectantly to see what it was that he couldn't understand. Was it something that we'd all overlooked? After all, we'd all successfully ordered from the same menu with no problems.

"Oh…err. Well, a roasted poussin is a young err… chicken that is err…roasted" the waitress began answering, to a background noise of sniggers from us lot before an increasingly agitated Knobhead shouted

"Yes, I bladdy know what a poussin is for gad's sake! It's this thing here" once more jabbing the menu but this time with more aggression.

"Oh...err. Well, salted radishes are...well, radishes that are err...salted." To guffaws of laughter from within the pub Knobhead snorted "Yes. OK. I suppose it'll have to be two of them."

On that note, my daughter and I retired to our accommodation for the evening, a comfortable unit situated directly to the rear of the pub. I'm happy to announce that we again slept soundly throughout the night and most definitely weren't disturbed by any chilling screams. I know what you're thinking. 'But why would you possibly have been disturbed by chilling screams Neil?' Well, take a seat and I'll tell you why...

Remember those 'Stewkey Blues' cockles that I was talking about earlier? Well, they have been harvested from the native mudbanks going back hundreds of years by (traditionally) the village's womenfolk. It was a hard, dangerous and exhausting job. But the men went fishing or worked on the farms and the women went cockling – that's how it was. One particular day, during the eighteenth century, the Stiffkey women went out as usual to trawl Blacknock to gather as many cockles as they could. One of their group was a young hard-headed and stubborn girl who went by the name of Nancy.

After a while the weather started to take a turn for the worse. As the tide started coming in, quickly filling up the creeks, a dense fog (known locally as a roke) began to enshroud the already bleak and hazardous landscape. The women were used to these harsh conditions of course, so packed up and started to head back to the safety of the village as a unit, to the warmth of their homes and families. All apart from Nancy. You see, the women got paid for every full sack of produce they returned with; an incomplete bag may result in not getting any money for the day.

Ignoring the pleas from her fellow cocklers she stayed out on the mudbank all on her own in a futile attempt to fill her sack. By the time she noticed how much danger she was in it was already too late. Unable to navigate her way back to safety she repeatedly called out in an increasingly desperate attempt for help, but it was to be all in vain. That dense fog meant her retreating workmates could sadly hear her cries yet could not locate her and dreadfully were unable to help. Local fisherman attempted to row out in their small boats but were also unable to find her, as the water got deeper and deeper, the fog thicker and thicker. Legend has it that as Nancy realised that she was not going to be saved her wretched screeches turned to spiteful curses against the grimly stark environment, the haunting roke, the cruel sea and even the good Lord himself. Then all at once she could be heard no more.

Tragically, Nancy's drowned body was discovered the next morning draped in seaweed, her eyes remained hysterically glaring from the injustice of what had happened to her. In one hand she was still holding the knife she used to collect the cockles, the other securely attached to the sack containing her incomplete haul.

Even though her body was laid to rest in the local graveyard, Nancy's moving spirit, to this day, is said to be out there on Blacknock mudbank…and on those nights when the tide eerily starts to come in, accompanied by that sinister roke, her noisy screams can be heard once more, along with those curses that she uttered with her last breath. Even more terrifyingly she has often been glimpsed through the fog, draped in seaweed with water pouring from her mouth, eyes wide open with that possessed stare.

Now don't you be thinking about wandering too far out there on your own onto the saltmarshes at night will you? You may just meet Nancy the Screaming Stiffkey Cockler…

Day 2 miles walked: 15.02 / Total miles walked: 30.94

STIFFKEY TO SALTHOUSE

I tell you what's underrated - a nice long soak in the bath, that's what. The relaxing feeling while you're taking one is totally undervalued, their soothing powers are completely unappreciated, the feel-good factor afterwards absolutely underestimated. While having a good old tubbing the previous evening I'd made a mental note to have a lot more of them once I'd returned home to Chesterfield after the walk. We usually go for the shower option, don't we? They're quicker, there's less faffing and they don't increase the monthly energy bill as much, I know. But I just felt so good afterwards.

I was still experiencing a niggly twinge around my left ankle but this was of minor concern as we headed up Hollow Lane and back towards the coast path. The full English breakfast that I'd just demolished back at the Red Lion had certainly added to my positive mood. Don't you just love it when they ask "How do you like your eggs this morning?" I always experience an overwhelming urge to wittingly answer "I like mine with a kiss!" just like in the jazzy duet performed by Helen O'Connell and Dean Martin. But I never do as I can always visualise the waitress willingly giving me a vigorous slap across the chops. Well, either that or walking back into the kitchen and saying to the chef "We've got a comedian on table 8. Idiot says he wants his eggs with a kiss" while simultaneously demonstrating the universally acknowledged wanker sign.

Anyway, I digress. As Leesh and I were walking up Hollow Lane we saw the local sports field to our right-hand side. I was pleased to see this as, the night before, I'd wondered where it was in the village while viewing some photos of the Stiffkey cricket team that were on display in the pub. You never know what's happened in the game do you when you see these after-match team pictures. Had there been a heroic innings from the local talisman enabling his team to knock off a winning total of 238 for the loss of three wickets or alternatively had they just got hammered after collapsing to an embarrassing 47 all out. 'Come on lads, smile. You'll soon be in the pub'! Without speaking to the participants we'll never know. They're always good to look at though and I have a passion for the ones where there's one team member who's looking in the totally opposite direction to the camera, like someone out of shot has just shouted to him "Albert, your wife's just ran off with the blacksmith!" or whatever they yell to distract someone in a sleepy Norfolk village while they're having a team photo taken.

Any person who's ever wielded a bat, to whatever standard, will dreamily view a deserted cricket field, as I did. You'll imagine being at the crease, the sun's shining, the wicket is hard and true, the outfield is like glass. The broad-shouldered fast bowler is thundering in towards the wicket with unbridled venom as the stumper and slip cordon crouch expectantly, way behind you. Shiny down one half, with seam exposed, the red missile is released at breakneck speed. It's the perfect half volley as your front foot instinctively moves forward to greet it, willow bat coming down in a perfect arc as you expertly caress the ball away all along the floor, precisely dissecting the off-side fielders while executing a superb cover drive for four glorious runs. The appreciative crowd warmly applaud the exquisite stroke as the umpire turns to face the scorer to signal the boundary when…

"Fuck I've just rolled my ankle again!" I exclaimed, on today of all days. For today was the dreaded SHINGLE day, the day when we would be rigorously tested on the SHINGLE beach between Cley and Weybourne. Everybody 'in the know' had been warning us about it, all the guidebooks I'd read had mentioned it. I had the feeling that there were probably even residents far away on the remote Ascension Islands who were aware of it. I must admit to having given it some extra thought and attention, as to the best way to approach it and attack it, in the weeks and months leading up to the challenge. The problem was, living in landlocked Derbyshire, there was just no way of replicating this type of surface during the many training walks that we had completed. Short of going up to the local builder's merchant and asking 'Can I plod up and down in that great big heap of gravel over there for a couple of hours please mate' there is just nothing like it and therefore no chance to practise and develop a beneficial technique. I also thought back to the first morning of the walk as we crossed over the bridge into Thornham. A couple, who were having a gentle morning stroll, approached us and asked if we were walking the coast path. As we both politely nodded "Yes" they screwed their faces up in unison, almost wincing by proxy for the obvious ordeal we would be enduring, before earnestly warning "Oooohhh get ready for the SHINGLE" ...and I'd just gone and rolled my ankle again. This time, I knew I was in trouble.

Alisha had noticed the stumble and gave me a concerned look. "What are you saying big lad? Are you OK to continue?"

"Yeeeaaahh" I lied. "I'll have walked it off in ten minutes!"

Why do we always think we can 'walk' things off, just like that? Broken leg with shard of bone poking through the skin? No problem. Just walk it off. Torn hamstring (the one where you can actually feel the muscle tearing as it's happening)? Ditto. Just walk it off. You'll be fine.

For those of us 'of a certain age' I blame the parents for this blasé and utterly over-optimistic attitude. As a child, after falling off my bike, I made my way home in agony in floods of tears, bawling like a baby. My dad's response was "Bloody ell. Wots tha bin doin nar? Cum ere then and let's av a luk." He then spat on the palm of his hand before abrasively rubbing said saliva on the large area of my exposed thigh that was now skinless (with tiny fragments of stone embedded for good measure) then clipped me round the back of my head, all in one swift, seamless movement. "Tha'll be rate nar. Goowhon, bugger off and play befor I gi thee summat to cry foh. Oh, an don't forget to be omm early fo thi tee cos thee mam's art at seven to waste more munny up at t'club."

For those of you who do not speak Cestrefeldian this roughly translates as: 'Now then little fellow. That looks a nasty injury you have there. Let me see if I can help. There, there. You should be fine now. Would you like to carry on playing with your pals now? If so, could you please remember to be home early for your tea as your mother is going out to play bingo. Thank you. Love you'.

Requesting that we operated at a slower pace than we had on the first two days I began to 'walk it off' cautiously, very cautiously. My eyes were totally glued to the surface, optimistically hoping my left foot met the floor truly, with no pain. I would not be appreciating the stunning view of the saltmarshes this morning. The strictly adhered to modus operandi was to be head down, crack on and, yep, 'walk it off'.

Shortly before arriving in Morston (which seemed to take blumming ages) I noticed a lady who was throwing a ball into the creek for her dog. I uttered "Good morning" but my heart wasn't in the greeting, although I couldn't help but notice, with envy, the agility and sprightliness of the dog as it continued to excitedly bound into the water to retrieve its toy. We continued around the corner for fifty metres or so only to find ourselves lost. Again. To our left was what appeared to be a grim-looking bog that may or may not have been drying out (we weren't going to risk finding out, no thank you) while straight ahead was a fence with a rudimentary hole in it that led straight into a farmer's field. There was no official Norfolk Coast Path waymarker or acorn symbol to guide us, not even sight of a well-trampled path to give us a clue. Nothing/zilch/zero. Alisha and I stared at each other, arms tentatively outstretched. "Where the hell do we go from here?" Neither of us had a clue. We may as well have been in the middle of Nicaragua. What a strange and discombobulating feeling.

To the rescue came the lady and her dog, with playtime now finished for the time being. Their names were Patricia Moore and Scout. "Can I be of any assistance?" breezily asked Patricia, before letting us down gently by telling us that many coast-path hikers suffer a similar fate at this precise spot. "Follow me to where I'm parked at the National Trust info centre and then you'll be back on track."

Patricia, who lived in nearby Field Dalling, told us the interesting (if somewhat sad) story of how the plethora of second-home owners in the area had resulted in many local settlements becoming ghost villages at certain times of the year, especially during the winter months when there were a lot less visitors to the area. We don't think about this type of impact on the local topography do we, when we're renting the holiday cottages. Scout, meanwhile, kept looking over his shoulder at the person hobbling behind him. I just knew he was thinking 'Come on slowcoach. Get a move on. I want my breakfast!'

At the car park we bid farewell to our saviours and gratefully (for me) sat down at a welcome picnic bench. It is fair to say that I had not managed to 'walk it off' as yet. As I plonked myself down it somewhat belatedly dawned on me that I should have consulted Phoebe Smith's book for guidance when we had been lost a few moments earlier. Yet, as I had been feeling sorry for myself, this had remained securely stored in my backpack. Let's have a look at what she wrote. *'In about half a kilometre comes a section where the ground is often so saturated that crossing it is not recommended. Luckily a gap in the fence on the right allows you to take a detour via a farm track, which returns to the path a few metres later, through another fence gap'*. She'd only gone and nailed it again.

Morston has one hostelry and this is called the Anchor Inn. Again, my daughter and I arrived too early to go in and sample their wares. The pub's website informs us that they are primarily a 'Fish and Chip pub' whose menu features many beer-battered items including line-caught cod, cauliflower nuggets and coriander & pepper squid. If I ever do get the chance to dine here, I can guarantee that I'll gladly order all three of those options on the same plate at the same time – sounds yummy to me. Photographs of the interior suggest customers have the choice of sitting in two main areas (that are either 'light and airy' or 'warm and cosy') from where they can choose ales from Woodforde's and Lacons.

This is all a far cry from the 1960's when Ann Mary Bullimore was the Anchor's landlady. At that time the side room of the pub was extremely popular in the area for the playing of music and doubled-up as a dance hall for traditional country-style dancing. In those days you would be able to enjoy Ann playing the piano to such local dance favourites as: 'Rig-a-Jig-Jig', 'Starry Night For A Ramble' and (listen to this for an absolute banger of a name) 'Tommy Make Room For Your Uncle'. They certainly don't make them like that anymore. There was also the 'Long Dance' which, when compared to the previous three, sounds rather tame doesn't it? However, please enjoy reading the following description of the dance's routine from Ann herself (as described to Peter Kennedy from the excellent MUSTRAD website): '*And you'd each take your partner, and you'd form a long row, like you do Sir Roger de Coverley. And then you start off; the bottom four would set across the hands and jig round, and then when the second part of the tune came, the bottom two would take hold of hands and run right up to the end of the rows and back again. Well, after you'd done three or four sets, about the fifth pair up would start again, so at the finish you'd four or five couples would jump the dance up and down together. See what I mean? That was how it was done. Well, we used to go on 'til everybody'd had a turn and you'd got right up to the top, and each time you'd finish one up, but when you got to the top you'd finish one down. See, each time. The partner next to you used to go either up or down, so that you all got a turn in time, running up and down the middle'.*

Well, I don't know about you but I'm just visualising all the dancers ending up totally knackered suffering with black eyes and split lips with the odd tooth being loosened here and there. As a result I bet Ann did a roaring trade selling plasters, bandages and tots of whisky purely for medicinal purposes. I can also imagine a typical conversation the following morning being "Didya see that useless blook from Warham wi' the two left feet larst noight? Daance loike a dickey he did. He didn' know wather he should've bairn up, down, round about do waa did he? He caught me on thur bridge've moi nowse wi' his alba as wal...and he ended with three taans to moi wun and he ain' even from Morston!"

After a refreshing cuppa from the National Trust café, accompanied by a home-made rhubarb and ginger flapjack, it was time to move on again. If truth be told I could quite easily have stayed on that picnic bench for a while longer; foot elevated on the bench with the weakish sun just doing enough to give me a warm and soothing glow. The adorable Alisha had other ideas however, enthusiastically cajoling me along. "Come on big lad, pull yourself up and let's get moving. It's only another mile and a half and we'll be at Blakeney!"

A mile and a half? Crikey. By the time I caught sight of the proud-looking Blakeney Hotel, it felt like we'd done at least five. The path had been extremely rutted in parts which had made for a precarious passage for myself with every little misplacement of my left foot causing issues with my ankle. We were still moving forward however, although I understood our pace had reduced considerably compared with that of the previous two days.

I soon received an unexpected boost as we began to travel in the general direction of Blakeney Point, followed by Blakeney Eye. Surprisingly the path had become quite busy (by far the busiest section we had encountered up to date) with dog walkers strolling along steadily taking in the alluring views, once again featuring the husks of decaying boats that had seen better days. A man hesitantly approached us and, while pointing his hiking pole at a random spot somewhere in the ether behind me, enquired "What's that big place over there in the distance and how long do you think it will take me to walk there please?"

I turned around and to my surprise he was referring to Wells lifeboat station. I'd not contemplated the fact that it could still have been visible to us from where we now stood. There was an initial look of terror on his face when I explained we'd passed through there at approximately lunchtime the previous day, before clarifying that we had stopped overnight in Stiffkey and not been walking continuously since then. What this had clarified for myself though was, dodgy ankle or not, we *were* continuing to make good progress and *were* still doing fine overall.

Have we mentioned place names yet and the local custom of pronouncing said place names in a totally different way to how an interloper would? Well, at this opportune moment I think we should because our next port of call was to be Cley-next-the-Sea. First of all it's worth pointing out that, despite its name, the village has not been 'next-the-Sea' since the 17th century due to land reclamation and the silting-up of the river channel. The suffix could quite easily be removed; well, either that or amended to something like 'Cley-which-is-hundreds-of-yards-away-from-the-Sea', although I appreciate that this would hack people off when they were sending Christmas cards to the village's residents. I do acknowledge and appreciate that Cley is nearer the sea than, say Wymondham (pronounced Windum) for example. I mean 'Wymondham-next-the-Sea' would be totally taking the piss, I can see that.

Anyway, now we've cleared that up let's get back to how we should say Cley. My natural instinct, and I'm sure I'm not on my own here, would be to pronounce it so that it sounded like the stiff, sticky and fine-grained earth that, when wet, can be moulded into shape before being dried and then baked to make pottery, ceramics and bricks – in other words, <u>clay</u>. But I'd be wrong, very wrong. You see, believe it or not, the correct way to say it 'in these parts' is so that it rhymes with <u>high</u>, or even <u>sky</u> for that matter. Now we understand that, I can see it only being a matter of time before I write to the local council suggesting an amendment so that the place name reads:

'Cligh-which-is-hundreds-of-yards-away-from-the-Sea-although-still-a-lot-closer-than-Windum'. I look forward to seeing the road signs.

I found the approach to Cley/Cligh/Cly (your choice but you know where I mean) quite frustrating. First of all, the village's iconic early-19th century windmill is visible from quite a distance away. This lures you into a false and almost cruel perception of nearly 'being there'. The irritation is that the path channels you in a rather significant loop towards it, where you are comfortably walking parallel with the sea before eventually and brusquely changing direction due south (and having studied maps of the route at length you are in no doubt that you have to pass the windmill in order to gain access into the village). At this specific point you also become well aware that, but for a re-routed river channel that is impossible to cross here, you would be able to continue straight along the coast path onto the SHINGLE beach without having to detour through Cley at all. Apparently, the River Glaven re-routing project took place during 2006 to help stop localised flooding by initiating greater variations in flow patterns and thus achieving greater control of the overall water depth. However, with my ankle throbbing (and bear in mind we now had nearly forty miles of walking in the legs) it all appeared unnecessary; the cynical and mean-spirited side of me inaccurately contemplating if the Environmental Agency, responsible for the detour, had perhaps been in cahoots with the local council to ensure more footfall within the village and subsequently greater trade for the local businesses.

Whether true or not, once into Cley Leesh fancied an ice cream while I fancied getting my feet up. An A-board outside the Harnser café bar on the High Street enticingly advertised 'Norfolk Ices Served Here' and we both thought 'that'll do' but for different reasons. With no real ales on sale I surprised myself by opting for a bottle of water. In one hand my daughter gleefully accepted her selection of ices in a lovely, tall and ornate glass; a long, narrow spoon in the other to devour it with. As we took our seats I was aware of a big chap studiously 'weighing us up'. Resplendent with a dark beard and wearing an off-white gansey, he had huge arms that remained resolutely folded in front of his ample girth. Just think of Popeye's nemesis, Bluto.

Bluto: "Which way you heading?"

Me: "We're optimistically hoping to walk to Weybourne today before catching the Coasthopper bus to Sheringham."

Again, just like the couple in Thornham, Bluto demonstrated a knowing wince.

Bluto: "You know its SHINGLE?"

Me: "Indeed we do! Can you suggest any tips to make it any easier, like is it better to walk along the top of the main ridge or to stay landward and close to the marshes?"

Bluto: "Nope. You're fucked however you try to do it. Some people attempt the ridge, some try their luck closer to the fence. But there's no easy way to do it."

Great.

Me: "We were hoping that maybe the tide was going to be out so that we could walk along the solid sand."

Bluto: "Nope. Tide's in. You're *definitely* on the SHINGLE."

…and 30 minutes later we most *definitely* were.

As you walk on to the beach, and I kid you not, there is a rustic, almost inobtrusive sign that declares you are on 'PEBBLE BEACH'. 'No…shit…Sherlock', as someone once said.

The environment was otherworldly, the peculiar edge-of-the-earth feeling enhanced by a small fleet of looming, redundant, manky-yellow-coloured, monster-truck excavators that appeared to be standing 'on guard' behind a wooden, shed-like construction. The temperature had also plummeted from when we were in the village with a chilly spray dampening us, caused by the powerful incoming waves crashing against the stones. If a mob of one-eyed centaurs had started to emerge from within the tiers of SHINGLE I would not have been surprised.

However, other than my daughter, I could not see another living soul.

Leeshy looked at me, I looked back at her. I reckon she was secretly looking forward to the challenge as, with a grin on her face, she pleasantly inquired "Are we ready for this then big lad?"

I'd love to tell you that we then began 'walking' but the thing is, you cannot actually 'walk' on the pebbles. Stumble and stagger, that's what you do. It is not possible to put one foot in front of the other in the normal fashion as you cannot obtain any traction. Your legs appear happy to go up and down in an ungainly pumping action, where you only manage to propel yourself an inch at a time. At the same moment a peculiar soundtrack of crunching feet treading on SHINGLE creates a hellish association with the roaring cacophony of the sea.

After a while I turned around to see how far we had travelled so far – that wooden structure was merely 20 metres away. I suggested we moved away from the ridge and down towards the marshes. Maybe it would be easier to 'stumble and stagger' in that area? It wasn't, but on the plus side it was several decibels quieter as we became sheltered from the waves, plus we were now protected from the sea-spray.

I needed a focus to help me forget about what I

was doing; something to concentrate my mind from dwelling on my wearying thighs and calves, not to mention my pounding ankle that was clearly worsening. For once I wasn't even interested in the views. All I wanted to do was just get off the blasted beach as soon as I could, but deep down I realised I had at least another ninety minutes more on the unforgiving, unrelenting and energy-sapping surface.

My solution was to play the Pub-Name-Stomp. I thought of the hostelries I'd been in so far on the trip plus those I was still hoping to visit. In perfect time with my feet going up and down I commenced chanting: 'Mari-Ner, Mari-Ner, Wash-Tope, Wash-Tope, Orange-Tree, Orange-Tree' and so-on, and so-on, and so-on. 'Jol-Ly, Sai-Lor, Jol-Ly, Sai-Lor, White-Horse, White-Horse, Red-Lion, Red-Lion'. By the way, feel free to utilise this game if you're faced with a similar predicament.

Leesh broke the tedium. "Come on. Let's have a drink of water and a flapjack." It was a welcome break and possibly the best drink of water and piece of flapjack I'd ever had. Surprisingly we had made headway although the cliff protruding out of the beach at Weybourne Hope still appeared to be a fair way off on the hazy horizon. This didn't trouble me too much as, by now, I'd adjusted my target for the day. Instead of leaving the path at Weybourne, before going for a pint in the Ship, I'd already planned to skedaddle early at Salthouse and go to the Dun Cow.

We trudged on 'Life-Boats, Life-Boats, Lob-Ster, Lob-Ster, Red-Lion, Red-Lion'…and after a mammoth two hours and fifteen minutes on the SHINGLE we thankfully arrived at the point where we could turn off for Salthouse village, the Dun Cow and the bus stop for Sheringham (where we were staying for the night).

To put our time in perspective I can tell you that the distance between Cley and Salthouse, on the beach, is approximately two miles. This would take most able-bodied people, walking at a steady pace, about fifty minutes, or so. But I had been walking so slowly that it had taken me nearly three-times as long. For want of a better word I was bolloxed. I looked down at my ankle and, as expected, it had ballooned in size. It would be very interesting when I took my walking shoe off later in the day. As we approached the bus stop at snail's pace I announced to Alisha that I was unable and unwilling to hobble any further along the road to the Dun Cow. If I had to wait another 55 minutes for the hourly service, then so be it.

Thankfully the orange double decker approached us within five minutes. The service runs like clockwork. As it appeared in the distance it seemed to have a warm, reassuring glow surrounding it; almost halo-like…and a quarter of an hour later we arrived in the busy, ever-popular seaside resort of Sheringham.

This traditional, vibrant town is a Collings' family favourite along the UK coastline. It undoubtedly has a lot going for it including: an award-winning blue flag beach, a heritage steam railway, a theatre, a museum, a boating lake and a pitch and putt golf course. The attractive streets have a charming family-friendly feel to them and are proudly lined with independent shops, cafes and restaurants. More importantly though, there is also the Lobster pub, which just happens to be Alisha's preferred watering (or should that be 'cider-ing') hole there.

Originally an 18th century coaching inn, this quaint multi-room pub, featuring a couple of log fires, is adorned with antique fishing paraphernalia such as lobster pots and fishing nets while, on closer inspection, it transpires that the ceiling is decorated with old nautical maps. For those warmer summer months there is also an attractive outdoor area where you can relaxingly sup your ale while watching the world go by.

Three real ales were available, these being Adnams Ghost Ship, Greene King Abbot Ale and Woodforde's Wherry. I selected a pint of the latter. A 3.8% amber ale, it's fresh and zesty and just what I was looking for after a tough day of rambling. With my foot resting over the top of a strategically placed stool I felt rather content, even though my ankle did feel like there was a colossal pulse striking through it. Leesh, meanwhile, was carefully selecting from an impressive array of six traditional ciders that were in boxes nestled to the right of the bar. After she had sat down we began to reflect on our journey so far, deeply satisfied with the overall experience and the mileage completed. The weather had been fantastic, the views sensational, the company sublime. The elephant in the room, of course, was my injury and could it stand up to the challenge of another day…

We decided that we were going to dine in the Lobster, but as the kitchen was having a break until five o' clock we would just have to quaff more beer and cider for a little while longer. I know, I know - it's a tough life. What always impresses me about the place is how laid back it is and that you do not have to be in for very long before you can be engaged in splendid conversation, if you want, with an eclectic mix of locals that also includes the friendly bar-staff. Nothing too serious and in my experience there's been no mention of race, politics or religion which suits me just fine.

The pub, no doubt, has experienced its fair share of palavers in the past, just like every other hostelry in the land. For example, on Saturday 3rd September 1938, a local named Mr Reginald Pegg of Gun Street (there remains a gaggle of Peggs residing in the town to this day) thought it a good idea to sweep his arm across the bar, damaging glasses and a biscuit jar, using foul language while doing so, after being refused service at 10:30pm. As the broken glass hit Mrs Winifred Coles (possibly the wife of landlord Ernest Arthur Coles), her daughter and a barmaid, he was ordered to vacate the premises. Refusing to leave, the police were called with the aggressor subsequently ejected. The drama didn't end there as, an hour later, Mrs Coles was accused of smashing a window at Pegg's house. A relative, Robert Pegg, recounted that he had seen her throwing four or five cream jars at the window. She admitted to throwing a single jar at the wall due to his wireless blaring loud and had not struck his window at all. After being summoned on Monday 12th September, Pegg was ordered to pay 10 shillings for each of the three offences and a further 3 shillings for costs. The case against Mrs Coles was dismissed.

I can confirm that there was no glass smashing, foul language or punters being lobbed out on our most recent visit to the Lobster, just a feeling of calm. In fact, to complete the picture of relaxation and cosiness, I watched as a man sat down in the window seat with a cup of tea, then proceeded to read a book before casually taking off his shoes and socks and having a snooze. Nobody batted an eyelid.

The food (Baked Crab for Leesh, Norfolk Blue Burger for me) was exceptional and rounded off another excellent session in this beloved establishment.

We were staying the evening in Mount Lavinia B&B on the Cromer Road and what should have been a steady ten-minute walk turned into a thirty-minute ordeal. After the three hours spent with my foot elevated in the pub the ankle had now totally seized up. The swelling had enlarged to a worrying size with the pain unbearable now I was on the move again. The adorable Alisha thoughtfully ran ahead to a convenience store to purchase a bag of ice. I anticipated I would shortly be undergoing the RICE (Rest, Ice, Compression, Elevation) self-care method.

After a seamless check-in I gratefully entered our room and collapsed onto the bed. Painstakingly removing the shoe from my humming foot as gently as I could, this only released an excruciating blast of pain. I immediately felt nauseous and began to shiver. My daughter was trying her best to get me organised, very very gently placing my leg on top of three pillows and ordering me to take a couple of ibuprofen tablets, for starters. She then wrapped a towel around the ice and swathed this around the problem area.

"AAAARRGGHHH...TAKE IT OFF...TAKE...IT... OFF!!!" It was far too heavy. I was in agony. She reduced the weight but it was still too much for me to bear. I was obviously aware that for the swelling to reduce I needed to have the ice on my ankle, but I just couldn't take it.

"Dad, you've got to have it on. If you don't how are you going to improve?" asked my daughter. "How are we ever going to be able to carry on with the walk?"

I went for Plan B which was to ask her to put me a bandage on...

Then I asked her to pass me my inhaler as I was feeling wheezy...

Then I asked her to close the bedroom window as the sound of the traffic was bugging me and giving me a headache...

Then I asked her to move my walking-socks away from my jumper as I didn't want it to smell...

Then I asked her to pass me a bucket 'just in case'...

Then I asked her to close the bathroom door as the whirr of the fan was making me feel anxious...

Then I asked her to..."DAAAAD!!! For god's sake!!! Just try to get some sleep!!!"

My needy self was running her ragged.

"OK Leesh, just leave me to it now. I've had some tablets, my ankle is compressed, my leg is raised and I'm resting. Let's just see how I am in the morning."

It was going to be a long night. I knew, in all probability, the only place I would be going any time soon was the nearest hospital.

Day 3 miles walked: 12.28 / Total miles walked: 43.22

SHERINGHAM TO CROMER

Dinah Washington once hinted to us *'What a Diff'rence a Day Makes'*; her golden-rich, powerful and emotion-packed voice stressing that it can be pissing it down one day only to be shortly followed, just 24 *liddle* hours later, by the sun beaming down, gently encouraging brightly coloured flora to sprout up 'all over the shop'…well, maybe not exactly in those words but you get my gist. For me, it was the change that could be experienced after one single night between the sheets. Admittedly, by no means did I manage a solid eight hours asleep – I stirred part way through to take some more anti-inflammatory/painkiller tablets – but ultimately, I did awake in a lot better shape and mood than I'd experienced the previous evening. The pain had thankfully eased somewhat and it was encouraging to see that the swelling had reduced. Carefully unravelling the bandage and replacing it with a towel full of ice, I metaphorically put on my strongest pair of big boy pants and tried to figure out, in a positive manner, what my capabilities could be during the next few days.

Totally sure about one thing, I didn't want the walk to stop there, in Sheringham. Even though there was the injury, I was still delighting in the overall journey so much that I wanted one last hurrah before returning home. I really felt that there was a little bit more to give and fully expected my body to make one last sustained effort. The recognised halfway point of the coast path is Cromer with all its timeless charm, rich history and lively culture. Surely it wasn't beyond me to manage a 4 mile hobble across the cliff-tops before belatedly accepting my fate by calling a temporary halt to proceedings. We would then return home to Chesterfield and attempt the second half at a later date. It sounded like a plan to me. All I had to do now was get the idea rubber stamped after convincing my daughter. By the way, did I mention she's a health professional...

Nurse Alisha: "You worried me last night Dad. There's no way you're walking to Cromer. You're nowhere near fit enough and you could do yourself more damage. We're catching the train home, you can go and see a doctor, and that's that."

Patient: "Look Leesh, it's only four miles and if it takes me all day I'm going to give it a go. Strap me up and I'm sure I can do it."

Nurse Alisha: "What if your ankle totally breaks down on the cliffs and we have to call for emergency help?"

Patient: "I can slide to safety on my arse. That's not an issue. I'm going for it!"

Nurse Alisha: "You're an idiot."

…and with that, we headed downstairs for our continental breakfast.

I don't know about you, but I'm never enthralled when I see the words 'Continental' and 'Breakfast' together on a menu. Initially it always seems to me that the venue cannot be bothered to put in enough effort to cook any food and are therefore simply choosing a less arduous (and probably cheaper) option by providing some uninspiring cereals, bland breads and weak cordials. That morning, I had even contemplated giving the option a miss (even though it was included in the overall price of the room) and instead, grabbing something more substantially greasy at a local café. But this would have been a big mistake.

Rathan, the affable proprietor, was patiently waiting for us as we entered the comfortable dining area/kitchenette. He proudly provided an induction of the gleaming facilities including such items as toasters, toastie-makers, coffee machines and smoothie blenders. His 'pièce de résistance' was the impressive variety of food aesthetically displayed along a kitchen unit including yoghurts, fruit juices, hams, cheeses, a choice of breads, cereals, spreadable items including jams and peanut butter, pastries and an excellent choice of fresh fruit featuring vibrantly coloured, succulent strawberries.

'What did you select then Neil', I hear you asking. Well, let me tell you, I was in my element as I went for the buttered-crumpets-with-marmite combination, washed down with several refreshing glasses of 'tropical' flavoured fruit juice. What a treat!

To make my day, once I'd quickly ascertained that Rathan was of Sri Lankan origin (a couple of rooms are named after cities Colombo and Kandy), we had a wonderfully upbeat discussion about some of that nation's cricketing greats such as Sanath Jayasuriya, Muttiah Muralitharan, Kumar Sangakkara and Lasith Malinga. The host seriously impressed me with his back-catalogue of cricket shots (while brandishing a trusty hotel broom as a substitute for a bat), nimbly displaying an array of leg glances, on-drives and square cuts from the confines of his B&B, as he enthusiastically recounted how his country had won the 1996 World Cup Final.

Even though we'd only been at Mount Lavinia for the one night I'd really enjoyed my stay there in more ways than one. It was just what I'd needed. As the adorable Alisha eloquently described the experience, 'It was a homely environment without the uneasy feeling you're intruding in someone else's home'.

I knew it was going to be a good day as we made our way back through the town, heading towards the coast path for the last time this particular week…

I live on the fringes of the Peak District with much of this upland National Park being in my county, Derbyshire, before it expands into Cheshire, Staffordshire, Greater Manchester and the south-westerly areas of Yorkshire. The highest point is Kinder Scout measured at a majestic 636 metres. I know what a hill looks like, I know how it feels to walk up one and yet Beeston Bump (the first testing hill we'd encountered) caught me by surprise. I don't mean in a "whooaaahhh, what the fuck's this?" sort of way, like a bolt out of the blue. You can see the path stretching up towards it but, at 63 metres, it's still a stark challenge after the mainly flat or gently undulating terrain encountered so far. Thankfully, there are steps to aid you on the climb, a handrail if needed and a bench where you can take a breath and enjoy the Sheringham town landscape if you so desire. Once at the summit, the spectacular panoramic views from this vantage point are well worth the effort of getting there, looking out over the compelling North Sea vista.

It was very peaceful when we reached the top and yet, during World War II, it had been home to a hive of activity. The Beeston Hill 'Y' Station was a top-secret listening platform that was part of a chain of similar front-line locations for the War Office's Bletchley Park code-breaking operation. This specifically constructed Wireless Interception facility (the 'Y' distinction derived from the W and the I) was base for a crack team of female operatives for direction-finding on enemy wireless transmissions. Locating the opposition's U-boats became an especially critical task where these skilled technicians were able to detect the origin of their signals in as little as six seconds (where crucially, a German Admiral, Karl Dönitz, had advised his commanders that they would not be located if they limited their wireless transmissions to under thirty seconds). VHF radio signals, used by fast patrol German E-boats for short range voice communication and transmitted in Morse code, were also gathered. In a distinct sign of the times, these coded messages were written by hand on paper, then transported to Bletchley Park by despatch riders.

After the war the 'Y' stations were deliberately dismantled in an attempt to maintain the secrecy of the locations, and all that remains of this once-critical military intelligence gathering unit is its octagonal-shaped concrete base.

After descending the 'bump' we soon skirted a large caravan site where a few of the static vans appeared to be rather closer to the cliff edge than they perhaps once had been. This was the first occasion we'd really noticed the effects of rising sea levels on coastal erosion in this area, the sands of time slipping away for these crumbling eastern shores. There'll be more, much more, about this in later chapters...

You never know what you're going to find in this area. Just imagine this. You're taking a leisurely stroll along West Runton beach (situated approximately mid-point between Sheringham and Cromer) and, by chance, you notice a large bone protruding from the cliff face. This happened to Margaret and Harold Hems in 1990. Diligently, they contacted Norfolk Museums Service who identified it as the pelvic bone of a large Steppe mammoth.

About a year later, a local fossil hunter named Rob Sinclair discovered even more large bones resulting in an exploratory excavation taking place, subsequently followed in 1995 by a more thorough one that lasted three months, carried out by the Norfolk

Archaeological Unit in tandem with the aforementioned Norfolk Museums Service.

This exploration revealed 85% of a skeleton, believed to be the most complete of a Steppe mammoth ever found in Britain. Male in gender, he would have stood four metres tall at the shoulder, weighing in at around ten tonnes which is twice that of a modern-day African elephant. These remains were discovered in what is known as the 'Cromer forest-bed formation West Runton', a thick layer of organic-rich mud deposited during the Cromerian Interglacial Stage about 700,000 years ago. To put this into perspective it was long before the last Ice Age. The deposit was found to be teeming with a multitude of fossils including small snail shells, amphibians, birds and bones of other mammals, that are familiar to us in the UK now, such as deer and horses. Now listen to this. Ongoing discoveries have since revealed the bones of rhinos, bears, wolves, hyenas and elephants that were all roaming our country in herds and packs way back when.

Further finds along what is now commonly referred to as the 'Deep History Coast' have provided the earliest evidence for human occupation discovered so far in northern Europe at a mind-blowing 850,000 years ago, 350,000 earlier than had previously been thought (and there will be more on this later). Like I said earlier, you just don't know what you're going to stumble upon in these parts.

With my ankle holding up nicely, onwards we travelled along the cliff tops out of West Runton, bordering another sizable caravan park before joining the pavement alongside everybody's favourite coastal road. Yep, we were acquainted once more with the A149. Happily, it was a totally different version to what we'd experienced a few days earlier in the villages of Thornham, Brancaster and Burnham Deepdale. Believe it or not, on this stretch, vehicles were tootling along adhering to the speed limit in exemplary fashion. We'd obviously not spotted the roadblock operated by the local traffic police who'd effectively inoculated the local speedsters with a transformative tranquiliser. We were grateful for this manoeuvre particularly when sneaking our way along the narrow path through East Runton, where I was eager to pop into the Fishing Boat pub, just for a quick half.

It wasn't because I was attracted by the selection of ales, or by the offer of 'free pool', or that I was fascinated by the flint-based frontage to the building. No, it was because while doing my pre-walk research I'd happened across a picture of the establishment that had really made me chuckle. 'Why's that then Neil', I hear you ask. Well, I'll tell you why. There is a porch at the front of the hostelry featuring a central window with two blackboards symmetrically placed either side of this. On one of these there was a chalk written notice advertising that a part time cook was required within, 'ask at bar for details'. The thing that humoured me was, someone had slightly amended the second 'o' of 'Cook' so that the advert now read 'Part Time Cock Required'. Hilarious. I love things like that. I suppose it could have been a naughty young whippersnapper who could have altered the original, but I'd like to think it was an adult buffoon such as myself.

Eventually Leeshy and I trundled into the suburbs of our finishing location where we were greeted by a splendidly imposing, primarily green, roadside greeting proudly announcing 'Welcome to CROMER' in bright yellow lettering. We'd made it! Featuring the town's crest, it also informed us that Cromer is the 'Gem of the Norfolk Coast' and has 'Twin towns' of 'Crest (France)' and 'Nidda (Germany)'. It seemed an ideal place to have a celebratory photo taken and, in an act of supreme timing, a prospective photographer approached us in the shape of a local chap who was briskly going about his business.

Standing smack-bang in front of the sign I smiled and politely asked "Excuse me. Would you mind taking a photo of my daughter and I in front of the sign please?"

"What sign do you mean?" he answered.

"This one here, you total spanner" I almost said, before recovering just in the nick of time to respectfully point at the big metal thing that loomed over us. To be fair to him, I had noticed a minor sign a few yards away denoting 'Runton Road Car Park →' but why the fuck he thought we may want a photo in front of that will forever remain a mystery. Miraculously, against all odds, he managed to capture a decent image.

We advanced towards the town, up the slight hill and past the car park before heading down towards 'No 1 Fish & Chips' and the amusements on New Street.

It wasn't the adorable Alisha's first rodeo in this seaside resort and, as she paced ahead, I knew where she was making a beeline for – 'Davies Fresh Fish Shop' on Garden Street for a treat in the form of one of their largest dressed crabs. Now, Cromer is renowned for this delicacy with the townsfolk very proud of their links to the meaty and tasty crustacean and the 'Cromer Crab' branding, and yet what is unknown to most visitors to the area is that this really narks their near neighbours over in Sheringham. My mate 'life and soul' Paul, a resident of the Fine City of Norwich, amuses himself with this topic when visiting that town. He will casually point at a crab and ask "Are you sure that int from Crooma bor?" with the miffed proprietor always responding that it is certainly NOT from Cromer, thank you very much, and is definitely a Sheringham crab!

A similar question in Cromer (i.e. 'Are you sure that int from Sherinum bor'?) receives a totally different type of answer with the responder nonchalantly shrugging their shoulders, followed by a studious shaking of the head, almost as if to say there's no such thing as a Sheringham crab. Who knew there could be such rivalry over this Norfolk culinary delight that continues to captivate the tastebuds of many.

Anyway, enough of this frivolity. I guess by now you're wanting me to tell you all about the Grade II listed Cromer Pier…

Records show that an initial structure, most likely in the form of a jetty, was erected as far back as 1390. This was to provide a safe harbour for local seafarers, as well as a place for them to load and unload goods. Fast forward to 1582 and Queen Elizabeth I was granting rights to the locals to export wheat, barley and malt with the proceeds from such trade to be used for the maintenance and well-being of the pier (and the town of Cromer). Further progress was made 240 years later when a 210 feet-long, cast-iron jetty was built. This one remained for 24 years before being destroyed in a storm. Reverting to another wooden version, the builders went for a slightly longer replacement at 240 feet that soon became popular for promenading. Strict rules were implemented including no smoking, while ladies were required to retire by 9pm. In 1897 all leisurely strollers had to take an early 'retirement' due to a coal boat smashing into the jetty causing damage that was beyond repair.

Cromer was pier-less for the next 5 years until a new build – the one which we are familiar with to this day – was completed in 1902. Nearly twice as long as the previous one at 450 feet, the cost was £17,000 (I've heard from an 'expert' that, in current times, it would take contractors over 50 years at a cost of £170 billion...and the work would suddenly cease halfway to completion due to the government changing their minds on the length).

Due to its protruding position in the unforgiving and often brutally destructive North Sea, it has endured significant storm damage over the years, particularly in 1949, 1953, 1976 and 1978. Considering there have been several further setbacks, including a huge tidal surge that caused devastation in December 2013, it really is astonishing that it's still standing.

Classed as not only a local wonder but also a

national treasure, it is one of the county's most famous and endearing landmarks. A rare example of an unspoiled Victorian pier that continues to attract thousands of visitors every year, it is pivotal to Cromer's identity and culture. Crucial to the popularity is that it is one of just five UK seaside piers that has a fully working and flourishing theatre, and in this case it is home to the only remaining end of pier show, of its kind, in the world.

Sitting on the cliff top, with a commanding view over the pier and the sea in general, lies the Red Lion where we were staying the evening. Located on the junction of Tucker Street and Brook Street, as well as being an AA 4-star hotel it incorporates an award-winning bar that, on our visit, had seven local ales to choose from. These were: Grain ThreeOneSix (3.9% pale ale), Moongazer Norfolk Best (details unavailable), Mr Winter's Twin Parallel (3.8% session IPA), Lacons Vista, Lacons Legacy (4.4% blonde ale), Green Jack Trawlerboys (4.6% best bitter) and delightfully, one of my top tipples in the whole damn world, Green Jack Mahseer – at 5.8% a strong, bitter and very hoppy IPA. I celebrated (temporarily) finishing our ramble with a delicious pint, followed by another one, then another one, then…well, you can guess where this is going.

Specifically booking this accommodation as it

promised a 'sea-view', I'd envisaged myself triumphantly finishing a day of walking followed by a few pints, then a long, relaxing, soothing bath before reclining in a comfy armchair, feet up, staring out to sea. I'm pleased to report this is exactly what happened. In my right hand I'd also got hold of one of life's guilty pleasures...but 'titter ye not', as Frankie Howerd may have said. For, Ladies and Gentlemen, I am talking about the one and only Norwich Evening News.

I really love local newspapers. Wherever I am I always buy one, marvelling in 'what's on', what makes these places tick, what gives them their unique identity, what makes them special. For example, from the South Yorkshire area's letter writers featured in the Sheffield Star, there always appears to be strong feelings of 'outrage' at just about everything. In the North West's Liverpool Echo there's page after page of gangland related shenanigans. The Norwich Evening News comes into its own, however, with reports such as *'Man's fence blows down during gusty winds in Thorpe Hamlet'*. OK, I may have made that last one up but here are a couple of reports that have featured recently.

'Norwich: Puddle at Magdalen Road's Artichoke pub to be fixed'

At the very bottom of Magdalen Road in Norwich

(or very top of Magdalen Street, depending on which way you go at it) is situated the Artichoke public house. A distinctive 1930's flint building that was originally decorated in 'Brewers-Tudor' style, it features two impressive cone-shaped towers that were built to reflect the merlons (solid upright sections of a battlement) that had once flanked the nearby Magdalen Gate, a key part of the city's medieval defences. If you are visiting the city, and architecture is your thing, it's well worth a look.

In April 2023 Maya Derrick reported that a troublesome large puddle, that 'takes over' the busy pavement outside the pub, was to be finally fixed after 'causing a nuisance for decades'. You'll not believe this but, we find out that the puddle gets bigger 'every time it rains heavily', thus causing a bit of an obstruction for people who decide to venture that way.

To substantiate this article, to really give it some oomph, a photo of a local Labour councillor, Julie Brociek-Coulton, is incorporated. She is pictured teetering at the very edge of the offending puddle, thoughtlessly holding a carrier bag, when it is plain for all to see that what she most obviously requires is a snorkel and a pair of flippers. Alarmingly it also appears as though she is about to jump in.

Remedial work was to be funded from the

Councillor's £11,000 Highway budget. The good people of north Norwich could now sleep well knowing that they would no longer have to make the crucial decision whether to do the butterfly, breaststroke or front crawl before going for a drink in the Artichoke, Malt & Mardle or Kings Head on days when it had been wanging it down.

This is another one that caught my eye:

'Let there be light! Street lamp fury in the suburbs'

- 'Neighbours left in the dark over their street light'

Don't panic! Don't paniiiiic!!! There's a street light that's been out of use for two weeks in the Norwich suburb of Sprowston. Here we find local resident, Pauline Peters, disheartened that Anglian Water have not yet managed to turn a light back on after recent works carried out in the area. There is a photo (of course there is) of an indignant, hand on hip Pauline (resplendent in a red gilet), pointing at the raised source of illumination. To give credit where it's due, the street light appears to be unperturbed by the gesture. We learn from reporter Francis Redwood that Pauline, nearing the end of her tether, has even considered going 'up there' and fixing it herself before acknowledging that this perhaps wasn't her best idea. Thankfully for all concerned, there is (ahem) a glimmer of hope. An Anglian Water spokesperson was confident the issue would be resolved 'by early next week'. Phew, thank goodness for that, I can hear you all thinking. We can now all go back to concentrating on trivial matters such as the cost of living crisis, homelessness and global warming.

Starting to feel a little peckish it seemed an ideal time to take a recuperative, short stroll over to Mary Jane's Fish Bar. It was large cod, chips and peas for me; fishcake, chips and peas for Leesh. While enjoying our meal we looked back at our four days of walking and picked each other's brains for what we had learnt and what advice would we give ourselves if starting the walk tomorrow. This is what we came up with:

- Don't underestimate the mileage you have to walk. Hunstanton to Cromer is typically billed as being between 45-47 miles, and it may well be if all you do is rigidly stick to the coast path, pitching your tent on it at the end of the day. As you'll probably be heading off the official route to go for refreshments and for lodgings, consider the extra distance that needs to be factored in.

- Just because it is promoted as being a coastal walk don't think that you'll be hugging the seashore as you won't. Sometimes, particularly the stretch after Thornham to Brancaster, you'll have to keep reminding yourself what it is that you've signed up for.

- For novices/townies (such as Leeshy and I) bear in mind the differing weather conditions and the impact these can have on the subsequent terrains that you encounter. I'd read of the possibilities of howling winds, driving rain and severely muddy paths; we got sea breezes, sunshine and rock-hard tracks with tricky ridges to traverse.

- Always follow the official waymarkers and the 'National Trail' acorn symbols. *Spot the waymarker/acorn* can be a fun and obviously beneficial game. However, don't always expect to see either of them when you most need one (such as on the approach to Morston). On the other hand, when it's clear where you need to be heading (on the approach into Cromer, tell-tale pier stretching out into the sea with a huge church tower in the background) there are more signs than you can point a hiking staff at.

- Remember to treat the walk with the greatest respect. Phoebe Smith states in her guidebook that '*nothing worth having in this world comes easy'*. She's specifically on about the stretch of SHINGLE between Cley and Weybourne but I think this is an apt assertion about the walk in general.

"Come on big lad. Let's call it a day and get back to the Red Lion" said the adorable Alisha, spotting that my eyelids were beginning to get a tad heavy. "If you behave yourself I'll consider letting you have another Mahseer before you go to bed" and with that, the first half of our ramble along the Norfolk Coast Path came to an official close. If truth be told, I was already champing at the bit (ankle permitting) to start the next part…

Day 4 miles walked: 6.10 / Total miles walked: 49.32

After stocking up with an interesting selection of alcoholic beverages from the Co-op on the High Street, we took the train home the following morning. The first leg of the journey, Cromer to Norwich, was courtesy of the Greater Anglia train operating company. It's been a good year for them. They have a brand spanking new fleet of trains that cost a whopping £1.4bn (interesting stat here – it's the first time in living memory that a rail operator in the UK has introduced an entirely new set). They contain complimentary Wi-Fi, plug sockets at every comfortable seat and an industry-leading accessibility feature where there is no stepping up from/down onto the platform. The Automatic Vehicle Inspections System (AVIS) has been installed helping Greater Anglia to measure the wear and tear on the wheels. It also checks the condition of the brake pads, discs and the overall profile of the train itself, meaning that faults are swiftly identified and fixed promptly. Their punctuality record is second to none with some of the regional routes averaging a very impressive 98%. They also boast the lowest rate of cancellations in the UK at 1.4%.

The guard walks down the gleaming carriages with a minimum of fuss. There's a gentle and friendly prompt of "Morning everybody. Can I see your tickets and passes please" followed, after checking, by a "That's great. Thanks. Enjoy your day." No fuss or palaver, just quietly and effectively getting the job done. Passengers reciprocate this approach; they too are both relaxed and well-mannered.

The second part of the homeward trip, which takes us all the way back to Chesterfield, could not be more starkly different. Courtesy of East Midlands Railways, the two-carriage rattler awaiting us at Norwich Station looks like it has been hauled out of a Siberian salt mine. There's a cartoon dark cloud swirling above with Halloween bats encircling it. It's on its last legs. There's not a chance of any complimentary Wi-Fi or a plug socket at any of the tatty seats.

The sliding door into our dilapidated carriage wheezes open and the guard theatrically enters. Leesh and I both momentarily raise our eyebrows as he proclaims "LADEEES AND GENNELMEN. BOYZZ AND GIIIIRLLLLS. GET YOUR TICKETS AND PASSES READY PURRRLLLEEEAAASE! THIS IS A FULL INSPECTION." It's almost as though he believes he's landed a gig on the Orient Express. He checks our tickets with relish. "ALL THE WAY TO CHESTERFIELD HEY. AREN'T YOU THE LUCKY ONES! NO NEED TO CHANGE. IT'S ALL THE WAY THROUGH FOR YOU."

He carries onwards. "CAMBRIDGE TODAY! LOVELY. CHANGE AT ELY. CHANGE AT EEELLLYYY" followed by a "DONCASTER! FANTASTIC. GET OFF AT PETERBURRUGH FOR THERE" and on and on and on he went. Thirty minutes later we'd nearly reached Thetford before he'd completed his first inspection.

It is not all bad on here though. I must confess that there is one thing that I really do like about East Midlands Railways (specifically the Norwich to

Chesterfield route) and that is the impromptu onboard 'entertainment'. You never know what 'superstars' are going to embark. The manky rolling stock, similar to that of a freshly laid dog turd covered in bluebottle flies, seems to attract a certain type of character. Today is a classic case in point.

The train trundles through the weeds and other species of wildly growing vegetation into Peterborough station and I can see that the platform is thronged with prospective passengers, some who appear to be attired in fancy dress. Even for this journey it catches me by surprise, after all, it is only half an hour after midday.

I nudge Alisha and nod in the general direction of four ladies who are attired in Spice Girls regalia. There's the Scary one, the Sporty one, the Posh one and the Ginger one. Emma Bunton may or may not be disappointed to find that she is not represented. It is no shock when they park themselves in an empty four-seater opposite where we are sat. They are lively, vocal and, as they hastily retrieve prosecco bottles clinking out of a bursting Sainsbury's carrier bag, hell-bent on having a good time. Throughout the carriage I can see other people bedecked in costume although I don't think they are all part of a group who will be visiting the same destination. I sense this is going to be an epic trip.

As each bottle of prosecco is successfully opened there's a cheer of 'RAAAAAAAYYY!!!' by the girls in celebration. Corks ping and zing through the carriage like excitable asteroids, zipping and zapping off windows, headrests and light fittings. 'RAAAAAAYYY!!!' They're really getting into the swing of it now.

"Play some music!" says the Scary one to the Sporty one. Obviously, we all think this will be from the back catalogue of a certain 90's girl super-group, but which one will she play? 'Spice Up Your Life' maybe, 'Say You'll Be There' perhaps or possibly '2 Become 1'. We all look over in eager anticipation.

A massive curve ball is thrown as she plumps for the 50/1 shot 'Complicated' by Canadian pop-funkster Avril Lavigne. We didn't see that one coming. 'RAAAAAAYYY!!!' enthuse the girls. The verse is tentatively attempted; I'm not convinced they know all the words. The chorus is a different kettle of fish. They blast it out as though they are on the terraces of their favourite football team after a match-winning goal has just been netted. It's pure, unbridled joy. They are living their best lives.

'RAAAAAAYYY!!!' cheer the Spice-ettes as the track finishes. "Play it again!" prompts the Scary one, with the Sporty one happily complying. It is at this moment that the Ginger one turns to face me for the first time. I think she's looking for me to offer my approval. Her left eye glistens with happiness and joy but terrifyingly I notice her right one is twitching at me with a frenzied flicker. This gives her the menacing demeanour of an axe murderer. Is she sizing me up in anticipation of being her next victim? I'm honestly not sure so I avert her gaze and make polite conversation with Leeshy.

The track finishes for the second time. "Again! Again!" exalts the Scary one, to the surprise of nobody. However, the ladies are oblivious to the fact that trouble may be on the horizon. Making his way down the carriage towards them, and I kid you not, is a chap dressed as a traffic cone, magnificent in a white and orange-hooped guise (we find out later he's on his way to the T20 cricket match between Nottinghamshire and Derbyshire at Trent Bridge). I have a quick look at his friends who are sat a few rows down and spot a priest with a huge plastic crucifix, a cowboy and the obligatory pirate. They are pissing themselves with laughter as the exasperated Coneman exclaims "For fuck's sake. Can't you play something else. This track's doing my fucking head in!"

He's taken on a tough challenge. Even with one person (the Baby one) missing, the groups 'girl power' (thankyouverymuch) has not been diminished in any way. They are a formidable bunch; there are no weak links, no shrinking violets.

The Posh One: "Who the fuck do you think you are?" - shushing him away with the back of her hands.

The Scary One: "Fuck you Coney" - giving him the V-rods for added emphasis.

The Sporty One: "Are you some sort of Wannabe? Sit down Conewanker" – adding the middle finger.

The Ginger One, meanwhile, is smiling at him. Her right eye is twitching furiously at the anticipation of how easily she will be able to dismember him.

Coneman: "Look, all I want is for you to play something different. There's a million songs out there and you just keep playing the same fucking one. Please, put something else on."

The Ginger One: "Why don't we let this gentleman choose the next track." Holy-fucking-moly...she's on about me. Eye flashing like a stroboscope, she's going for the double – Coney and I with the same axe. I'm not prepared and am out of my comfort zone. I'm only a member of the audience. I'm in the process of stuttering a reply when a familiar voice comes to my rescue.

"LET ME PICK A SONG PURRRLLLEEEAAASE!" It's only our old friend who's decided to join the party, one of only a handful of people in the carriage who's dressed as he should be. It's the guard! "MAY I

SUGGEST EVERYONE'S FAVOURITE. AHEM. LET'S HEAR SWEET CAROLINE!"

'RAAAAAAYYY!!!' cheer all the passengers in carriage A, in unison. The request has gone down well. There's a slight hiccup as the Sporty One decides to play 'Hi-Ho Silver Lining' in error – "NOT THAT ONE!!!" – before we soon hear the familiar, and ever popular, tones of Neil Leslie Diamond. I mention to Leesh that I'm amazed this is not the official national anthem for England. It may well be one day; stranger things have happened. Everyone joins in, we're all swaying, hands in the air. We all know the words but it's our hero, the guard, who is stealing the show; he's taken his tie off, wrapped it around his head like a bandana and he's singing into an imaginary microphone! Ladies and Gentlemen, welcome to Great British Railways 2023 style.

Party classics continue to be sung with prosecco bottles clinking all the way into Nottingham station where the fancy dress people get off. East Midlands Railways have delivered once again. Their fares may be overpriced and their trains antiquated but, you have to admit, they can't half put on a good party.

Even if they don't know it.

SALTHOUSE TO SHERINGHAM

The adorable Alisha and I were back in Norwich for a weekend during July, to celebrate my birthday. We were joined by my wife, the delectable Denise, and eldest daughter, the pristine Paige. I love celebrating my birthday in the 'Fine City'. In fact, to be more specific, I love celebrating my birthday in the Fat Cat pub on West End Street. It never fails to hit the spot.

There's always a staggering amount of quality real ales to pick from plus, if you're feeling a tad peckish, there's quality pork pies on sale to fill that gap. It's twice been selected by CAMRA (Campaign for Real Ale) as their national pub of the year and continues to win a host of awards at a local level. The comfortable interior is bedecked with fascinating breweriana while there's also a couple of outside areas that are considerately covered to protect punters, who prefer to booze al fresco, from the elements. They even have their own Fat Cat brewery.

There we were on the Friday evening, having a jolly old time, with me contentedly tucking into my fifth pint of Fat Cat Marmalade (5.5% classic English strong bitter with a pleasing burnt citrus finish). All was well with the world as you can probably imagine.

Paige innocuously enquired as to when Leesh and I were going to undertake the second part of the Norfolk Coast Path. It was at this point it dawned on me that, for completeness, we'd also need to walk between Salthouse and Sheringham, this being the stretch we'd undertaken by bus because of my ankle issue...and as I queued at the bar to get another round in, I had a brainwave that as we were already in the vicinity we may as well do it tomorrow. No planning needed; no overnight stops to be booked. Let's get it done! I have some of my best ideas when I'm pissed, don't you?

Carrying the tray of drinks back to our table I excitedly relayed the good news to Alisha while also extending the invite to the wife and eldest daughter. For some inexplicable reason I sensed that none of them were sharing my enthusiasm for the task ahead.

The delectable Denise: "Not...a...chance Neil."

The pristine Paige: "No way José."

The adorable Alisha: "Do we reeeaaaally have to Dad?"

Me: "Yeah! It'll be brilliant."

The adorable Alisha: "Hmmmm. OK then. I suppose we've got to do it at some stage."

The following morning, we were stood outside the bus shelter on Sheringham's Station Approach patiently waiting for the Coasthopper to Salthouse. I was experiencing an uncomfortable hangover and idly musing if this could have been related to the amount of mustard that I'd daubed over a third piece of pork pie the previous evening. There was a slight and yet irritating drizzle in the cool, grey air and last night's bravado suddenly seemed absurd as I began to consider binning the walk and spending a few hours in the Lobster pub instead. I was then distracted by a lady (locked into a local travel app) stood behind me who was wittering on about which bus was going to arrive first – in a thrilling contest it was apparently neck and neck between the No. 44 and CH1 services. Initially, the 44 was ahead but had been surprisingly overtaken by the CH1. The lead changed hands again…and then again…and then again! It all got rather exciting as other people began to take an interest, theorising about what on earth could be 'gorn

orn' somewhere up on the Cromer Road. In crazy scenes there was a huge cheer as the CH1 screeched around the corner to receive the chequered flag. We all clapped enthusiastically and doffed our imaginary caps in saluting the driver who had obviously pulled off an exhilarating, last-gasp manoeuvre somewhere opposite the Tyneside Club on Station Road.

The driver looked at us all as though we were fucking crackers.

Fifteen minutes later he dropped Leesh and I off just past the Salthouse duckpond and we made our way back along the footpath towards Beach Road. Aided by a couple of bottles of H_2O, my hangover had disappeared and I was ready for the walk. I felt utterly, massively and totally different from the last occasion I'd been in these parts just a couple of months previously. This time I'd not got over 40 miles in my legs, this time I wasn't lugging a backpack about, this time the ankle was fine and this time it was on my terms. In fact, I never thought I'd think this but it was an absolute pleasure to re-acquaint myself with my old adversary, the SHINGLE.

There was the re-assuring, familiar 'crunch' sound with each progressive footstep made, accompanied by a backing soundtrack of breaking waves crashing onto the shore before fizzing their way back down the

SHINGLE and into the sea. As our pace quickened and the body temperature rose, the persistent drizzle felt refreshing. This was more like it.

We reached a fairly busy Weybourne Hope (where several sea-anglers were trying their luck) before leaving the SHINGLE, for the very last time, and headed up Gramborough Hill for a delightful stretch of walking on the cliffs. It's worth highlighting, at this stage, that the sea views over to our left were enthralling with the peppery sea air intoxicating. Not to be outdone, on the right-hand side (and as we edged around the local golf course) a steam train came chugging along the adjacent heritage railway line with vast plumes of smoke powerfully bursting forth into the Norfolk sky. It felt like we were walking through an enchanted kingdom.

A climb up Skelding Hill (170ft above sea level) brought us to the local lookout station at the summit. Sheringham Coastwatch is a totally self-financing charitable organisation manned by volunteers for 365 days a year. As you can imagine from such a height, it offers a commanding view that extends 15 miles out to sea as well as being ideally placed to observe the nearby beach and cliff paths. Being the eyes and ears of HM Coastguard in Sheringham, all commercial shipping, pleasure craft and other viewed vessels have their key details recorded such as: time of observation, type of vessel, name and number, the colour of its hull and superstructure, its true bearing and heading plus its speed and distance from the watchtower. Weather conditions are also recorded regularly including wind direction and force, the state of the sea, visibility, cloud cover and barometric pressure. The garnered information plays a critical role in supporting investigations into any incidents and emergencies as well as ensuring the overall safety of all sea and coastal users in the area.

As my daughter and I passed, we gave the chap who was on duty a cheery wave.

It was all downhill from there (in a good way) as we headed past the old boating pond towards the town. The nearer we got I began to notice impressive artwork on the sea walls. After a few yards one of them caught my eye. 'What was that then Neil', I hear you ask. Well thanks for enquiring. It was a painting of the one and only Albert Einstein sat contentedly on a large rock. He's wearing a white tea-shirt, blue shorts and brown sandals with a mug of tea at his side. Now, at this point you're probably wondering why on earth there's a painting in Sheringham of a German-born theoretical physicist who's widely held to be one of the greatest (if not *the* greatest) and most influential scientists of all time. Let me tell you the story behind it…

In 1933 Einstein (who was Jewish) was being persecuted by Adolf Hitler as the Nazi party came to power. He therefore had to urgently flee continental Europe (never to return) and, at the invitation of Oliver Locker-Lampson (a Conservative MP who he'd previously met and trusted), came to stay in a humble wooden hut on the secluded Roughton Heath near Cromer. Although his stay in Norfolk only lasted three weeks, protected the whole time by armed guards, it is believed to have been a seismic moment in his life, a sort of crossroads. Prior to his visit he was an avowed and ardent advocate for non-violence and pacifism. Yet, at the end of the three weeks he gave a speech to 10,000 people at the Royal Albert Hall emphasizing the existential threat to European civilisation and that this must be fought against. Shortly afterwards he emigrated to the United States of America, living the rest of his life in exile.

The sight of Einstein, on that innocent sea wall, got me thinking. You see, everyone is so aware of his intellectual achievements and originality (for example, his mass-energy equivalence formula $E=mc^2$ has been called the world's most famous equation) that the name *Einstein* has become synonymous with genius. It is a fact that his name is so well known that it is widely used by the general public in a certain situation. For example, if someone is asked a particularly tricky and testing question that they have no chance of ever answering correctly, they will generally answer 'Not a clue mate. Who the fuck do you think I am, Einstein?' I'm not sure if the esteemed scholar would have been impressed with his surname being utilised in this way but I think it's a fantastic achievement.

As my daughter and I wandered through the door into the Lobster for some post-walk beverages, I pondered who else has been informally awarded this type of accolade. Well, I am aware that I've used a couple in this book already. Firstly, one of the most successful Formula One Grand Prix racing drivers of all time, Lewis Hamilton, got a mention as an exaggerated comparison to the A149 speedsters in Brancaster.

Can you remember the second example? I always find this person particularly random to be quoted as he is a fictional character. It's everyone's favourite consulting detective of course, Sherlock Holmes, famous for his proficiency with observation, deduction and logical reasoning that borders on the incredible. His name is sarcastically used (as in 'No shit Sherlock') by someone when faced with something that is extremely evident. In my case it was to emphasise the obviousness of the 'PEBBLE BEACH' sign when entering the shitload of SHINGLE at Cley.

I'll just mention one other. My mate Paul Sweeting was persuaded by his missus to go into a glitzy bar during a trip to London. For two cocktails the bill was £30. After the drinks (which were very nice apparently) had been polished off she asked if they were going to have a second. His reply was "Not at these fucking prices…who do you think I am, Rothschild?" Used rhetorically, this is often said by someone to emphasize their own dearth of finances or status in comparison to a family whose name is historically associated with immense wealth and influence.

You will undoubtedly be aware of other examples that I have not mentioned so feel free to play this game at home folks…

The girls behind the bar in the Lobster remembered us from the last time we had visited. They even asked if we'd been out walking again. I'm always pleasantly fascinated when people display excellent memory skills as I often cannot recall what I've had for my breakfast.

Did you know that the mechanism for memory is unknown? We do know that there are two types of memory, these being short-term and long-term. Short-term (also referred to as 'working') is generally considered to be what we use day-to-day, where we keep information while using it before either discarding it or transferring it to our long-term storage capabilities. Long-term is related to what we did in the past, sometimes going back many, many years. It is the place where our brain stores the information that we want to keep.

Did you also know that there is a question about whether the issue with memory is in retaining the information or being able to recall it? Taking a common-sense approach a distinction is probably unimportant in practice. After all, to produce the information we surely need to have retained it before ever being able to recall it, don't we?

Finally, did you know the most important thing that we can do to maintain our memory is to keep healthy? Eating a well-balanced diet, having between seven and nine hours sleep each night, undertaking a regular physical exercise regime and keeping stress under control (the phrase 'my mind went blank' is associated with stressful moments) are all beneficial. It goes without saying that we are well to avoid using illegal drugs excessively. Alcohol can also prove to be problematic.

Anyway, now we've cleared that up where was I? Ermmmm.... Oh, I remember; the girls behind the bar having an excellent memory. We had an enjoyable chat about where we'd been that morning, the weather conditions encountered and how far we'd walked in total, that sort of thing. It was all very nice, some would even say convivial, if they could remember the word of course.

My phone rang and it was the delectable Denise who notified us that the pristine Paige and her good self were no longer going to join us in Sheringham as they had decided to stay in Norwich for an afternoon's spell of retail therapy. This was not a problem. Leesh and I simply relaxed with another couple of drinks in the Lobster before we caught the train back into the city to meet up with them in the Coach and Horses on Thorpe Road.

A five-minute walk around the back of Norwich railway station, the 'Coach' is a behemoth of a boozer. Bought by David and Rosemary Blake over 30 years ago in 1993, it had been closed for a couple of years and was in dire need of a refurb before the doors could be re-opened to the public. They are still the landlords to this day.

The onsite Chalk Hill Brewery (named after the surrounding area to the rear of the building) was also formed in 1993 by David and two of his friends, Bill Thomas and Tiny Little who all shared a passion for sailing and beer. Amazingly, this is now the longest running independent brewery in Norwich. The beer range includes Black Anna (4% milk stout), CHB (4.2% best bitter), Gold (4.3% golden ale), Dreadnought

(4.9% ruby ale) and Ruby (5.5% red ale), all of which take pride of place on the bar and can be served in four-pint jugs if you're feeling thirsty enough. Guest ales have also made an appearance in recent times.

Situated very close to Norwich City FC's Carrow Road ground, it is always rammed on a matchday, with both home and away supporters. Renowned for its selection of ales, reasonably priced and freshly cooked food (including delicious Sunday roasts), large outdoor beer space and roaring fire in the winter, it always tends to be on the busy side anyway.

Dogs are welcome with well-behaved humans...as are birds! Yep, there's a bloke who regularly brings his parrot (a very friendly and talkative chappie called Toby) to the pub for an afternoon sesh – that's the bloke, not the feathered creature in the cage.

We had a really good couple of hours there; you can't beat quality family time can you? I remember that we chatted non-stop, we reminisced, we laughed, we ate some lovely food and inevitably we quaffed more ale and cider. Then we retired to our accommodation for a well-earned and much needed sleep.

We were staying the weekend in an atmospheric apartment (a favourite of the family) situated on Saint Martin at Palace Plain. It is overlooked by Norwich cathedral, this historic treasure and iconic landmark rising high above the city's skyline. I awoke to a cloudless blue sky, the sun already beaming down, and went outside to take advantage of this wonderful start to the day. I'd got the Norwich Evening News with me (of course I had) and sat down on the public 'book bench' situated a few metres beyond the front gate.

The 'VisitNorwich' website explains that Norwich is a UNESCO City of Literature and has been a literary city for over 900 years. It has a thriving community of authors, poets, historians, novelists and story tellers and is home to the National Centre for Writing (situated within Dragon Hall on King Street) where people can share, learn and collaborate. To celebrate the UNESCO status, nine book benches have been erected across the city (including a 'bonus bench' at the University of East Anglia) encouraging people to meet, dwell and enjoy the sights and sounds. Made of stone, wood or metal, the beautifully designed benches are inspired by books; some are open as if marking the place you want to pick up next, some are piles of books with engravings depicting famous authors from the county, others are books waiting to be chosen from a shelf, one is resting on its spine with open pages to sit on. The one I was sat on was the largest of them. Designed by sculptor Ryan James it showcases a three-metre-long stone book incorporating 25 smaller books, each engraved with names of books that have a relationship with Norwich.

As I settled down to read the 'editorial' in the local paper I suddenly remembered that, the previous evening, I had been ordered by the family to ring the White Lion to book us in for lunch. I glanced at my watch (9 o'clock-ish) and made a mental note to give them a call an hour or so later. Not long afterwards I received a message from Alisha on the family's WhatsApp group chat instructing 'Dad don't forget to book White Lion for lunch☺xxx'. I immediately replied 'I'm on it Leeshyyyyyy!!!'

The last message was instantly followed by one from the pristine Paige. It said 'OMG WHAT THE HELL IS WRONG WITH U 2???!!! DAD YOU BOOKED THIS LAST NIGHT WHEN IN COACH&HORSES!!!'.

I sat back on my book bench and listened to the cathedral bells. I tried hard to recall the conversation when I was alleged to have called the White Lion but to no avail. My mind had gone blank. My short-term memory had failed to retain the details. How strange and yet how intriguing. I started to go through the list of items that we know encourage a healthy memory:

I'd eaten good quality food the previous day, briskly walked five miles along the coast thus topping up my fitness levels, slept for a solid eight hours, definitely not taken any illegal substances and didn't feel the least bit stressed. That can only leave one thing...it must have been that intoxicating Norfolk sea air!

Day 5 miles walked: 5.50 / Total miles walked: 54.82

HOPTON ON SEA TO CALIFORNIA CLIFFS

Right, get your pen and paper ready because I want you to make notes about the best way to purchase rail travel. Are you all set? Good. Firstly, <u>DON'T</u> go to the railway station on the day of your journey and buy your ticket there and then. <u>DO</u> plan in advance, as far back as you are able, and jiggle the stations about that you know you'll be travelling through, **and stopping at**, in order to obtain a better deal (the experts call it 'split-ticketing'). <u>DO</u> purchase a railcard if you are eligible as this will get you a third off the initial price (I have a 'senior' one, Alisha a '26-30'). Here follows what I did and how much I ultimately saved for our next two train journeys: Chesterfield to Norwich (1st October 2023) and Cromer to Chesterfield (5th October 2023). The fare shown is the cost for two tickets, booked 22nd August 2023.

Journey #1 Depart Chesterfield 11:00 / Arriving Norwich 14:26

Initial Price **£194.00** (no railcards/no split-ticketing)

Actual Cost **£38.20** (using railcards and split-ticketing)

Instead of booking Chesterfield to Norwich, I split our tickets as follows:

Depart Chesterfield 11:00 / Arriving Nottingham 11:32. Cost **£9.90**

Depart Nottingham 11:43 / Arriving Peterborough 12:48. Cost **£14.10**

Depart Peterborough 12:52 / Arriving Norwich 14:26. Cost **£14.20**

Saving £155.80

Journey #2 Depart Cromer 09:54 / Arriving Chesterfield 14:19

Initial Price **£207.80** (no railcards/no split-ticketing)

Actual Cost **£37.90** (using railcards and split-ticketing)

Instead of booking Cromer to Chesterfield, I split our tickets as follows:

Depart Cromer 09:54 / Arriving Nottingham 13:37. Cost **£25.70**

Depart Nottingham 13:45 / Arriving Chesterfield
14:19. Cost **£12.20**
Saving £169.90
Total Savings £325.70

———

Three hundred and twenty-five pounds and seventy pence saved. Isn't that absolutely astonishing? Just for doing a little research, just for taking a little bit of time. That'll help to pay for a few beers. You're welcome.

Alisha and I arrived back at Norwich (Thorpe) railway station on Sunday 1st October, on schedule, for our third and final session of our Norfolk Coast Path ramble. The 2 weeks leading up to the trip had been fraught with issues on both personal and logistical levels. Personally, believe it or not, I'd had acute diarrhoea for a whopping 12 (TWELVE) days that had only abated 72 hours before the day of travel when, in an act of desperation (and against my better judgement), I'd taken some over-the-counter medication. I'd been trying to get through to my local GP, for advice, for days and had all but given up hope of speaking to someone. Deep down I knew I should let my body deal with the bug the best way it saw fit, but I was totally fed up with discharging everything immediately after ingesting it. I was tired, grouchy, had no energy and was rapidly becoming a shadow of my former self. Of course, as soon as I'd swallowed the tablet I successfully made contact with the surgery - the 'law of Sod' and all that or even one of 'life's little ironies' as Thomas Hardy was keen to highlight. They advised me in no uncertain terms to not take any pills to stem the tide and just let the virus run its course; I should continue to 'blast the windows out', so to speak.

Logistically, I had been made aware that train journeys on this day could be disrupted due to ongoing strike action by rail staff. However, as it happened, I had no need to be concerned as our journey ran on time.

We were staying our first evening in the Premier Inn that is situated just a short stroll opposite the rail terminus and across the Foundry Bridge that spans the River Wensum. Thousands and thousands of people traipse over this crossing into Prince of Wales Road without ever giving the structure a second thought or even a glance, hell-bent on getting to their destination whether that be for business or for pleasure. It is well worth a look too. Originally constructed in 1810, the current Grade II listed version dates back to 1886 and is made of stone, cast and wrought iron. It features rusticated abutments that have stone piers with moulded caps at each corner that all imposingly bear shields with the arms of the City of Norwich. It also includes a curved spout (thoughtfully added in 1910) through an upstream parapet that allowed thirsty steam lorries to draw water from the river. I guess it's no surprise to learn that an iron foundry once stood on the site of where the Premier Inn now stands.

My daughter and I rolled up to the hotel reception to check-in. We were in good spirits knowing we had the rest of the day to enjoy by, no doubt, imbibing a few ales at a local hostelry. The time was 14:40.

Me (cheery face): "Hi! We've got a reservation for a twin room for one night please…surname's Collings."

Receptionist (solemn face): "Check-in is not until 3. Would you like to pay £10 for an early one?"

Me (cheery-ish, but growing slightly inquisitive, face): "Errrrr, is our room actually ready?"

Receptionist (glancing at her screen): "Yes it is. But you can't have it until 3. If you don't want to pay the £10 you could always leave your luggage here, go and do some shopping maybe, then come back later?"

Me (incredulous face): "So you're telling me our room is available but to have it just 20 minutes early incurs a £10 fine?"

Receptionist (back to solemn face, I'm guessing it's not the first time she's had such a conversation): "Yes."

Me: "No chance am I paying that. We'll wait here in reception thank you."

Receptionist: "I'd prefer it if you moved away from this area as it will soon be very congested."

...and do you know what, it was, with other disgruntled prospective residents all refusing to pay the £10 for having the temerity to try to check-in twenty, then fifteen, then 10, then five minutes early for rooms that had already been cleaned and were vacant. With the clock creeping towards the magic time of '3' customers were spilling out of the door that led back towards the car park. Others were occupying the ramp that funnelled down towards the restaurant.

It wasn't exactly outright chaos, but it was that typically shambolic and slightly tense British scene that we're all familiar with (at airports, train stations, bus stations and yes, hotel check-in desks) where usually mild-mannered people - hindered by a host of suitcases, bored kids and a plethora of brightly coloured neck pillows - begin to mutter under their breath and sigh rather loudly. If they're from South Yorkshire they may even be contemplating penning a letter to the Sheffield Star to register their 'outrage'.

An imaginary klaxon sounded 'AWOOGAAA' but only in the ear of the receptionist (who now sported a smiley face). As if by witchcraft she was immediately joined by a colleague (also smiley face) who casually asked "OK, who'd like to check-in?"

There wasn't exactly a stampede, but it was yet another typically British scene that we're all familiar with where people begin to edge forwards without fully committing to the task as they don't want to offend anyone. Leesh and I were guilty of this as we hesitated ever so slightly, but it was enough to demote us into fourth place in the queue. Not too bad you may think. However, the check-in process is not necessarily slick at a Premier Inn and another 15 minutes had gone by before it was our turn.

Receptionist (smiley face): "Welcome to Premier Inn! Are you looking to check-in today?" Had she never seen me before?

Me (sarcastic smiley face): "I've been looking to check-in with you since twenty to three. With that in mind, and considering it's nearly twenty past three now, do I get a £10 refund for you checking me in 20 minutes late, by any chance?"

Receptionist (smiley face): "I'm not sure it works like that haha!"

Me (neutral face): "I'll take that as a 'no' then."

Receptionist: "Will you be dining with us tonight Mr Collings?"

Me: "No."

With check-in eventually navigated we swiftly dropped our bags in the room and made tracks to the Fat Cat and Canary pub on Thorpe Road. Originally named the Mustard Pot, after a steam tugboat that belonged to local company Colman's, it was re-furbished, re-named and then re-opened in 2012 as a sister pub to the Fat Cat. The addition of 'Canary' to the Fat Cat name is a nod in the direction of Norwich City Football Club (nickname: The Canaries) that is situated just a short walk away on Carrow Road. A splendid array of ales is available featuring several from the Fat Cat brewery range plus interesting 'guests' from around the UK. As well as comfortable seating in the interior there are also outside terraces to the front and rear.

In addition to the excellent beers to select from, the pub has also earned a glowing reputation for the artwork featured on its exterior. First of all in 2021, a mural dedicated to Daniel Farke (who was, at that time, the head coach of the local football team) featured strikingly on the main side-wall of the hostelry. This was in recognition of the German's second championship winning triumph of his tenure at the club. A couple of years later, and after Farke's appointment as boss of Norwich's league rivals Leeds United, landlord Christian Hodgkinson decided it was a suitable time to source a replacement painting...and what an inspired choice he made.

The new one is dedicated to Justin Fashanu, a star player of the club from the late 1970's/early 1980's. Scoring regularly for Norwich (and often spectacularly – a stunning effort against Liverpool in February 1980 won him the BBC goal of the season award) he managed a total of 40 goals in 103 appearances before becoming the first black player to be transferred for a £1 million. He was also the first professional footballer to publicly 'come out' as gay. Dying aged just 37 he was inducted into the National Football Museum's Hall of Fame in 2020. His legacy today extends way beyond his chosen sport and the mural is a wonderful tribute to an iconic figure in both football and LGBTQ+ history. It warms the cockles of my heart to see Christian celebrate Justin's life in this way.

If you pay the Fat Cat and Canary a visit don't forget to go around the back of the pub as there are two more wonderful paintings taking pride of place on a couple of garages there. These also feature much-loved Norwich City FC legends, namely Jeremy Goss and Grant Holt. All the paintings mentioned are the work of the hugely talented, professional local artist Dave Nash who has the working name of Gnasher Murals.

The adorable Alisha and I went inside the pub and ordered our drinks. She opted for a pint of rhubarb cider while I chose…yep, you've guessed it, a pint of Fat Cat Marmalade. 'Spin Sunday' was the entertainment – this is where local chaps come in and 'spin' some funk and soul vinyl records on their decks. Today it was DJ Chris who played some absolute belters. What a fantastic way to spend a Sunday afternoon, drinking quality ale in a quality establishment while listening to quality tunes. We stayed for a few hours before sensibly calling it a day. As we were about to leave I had a good chat with Chris, telling him we'd really enjoyed our afternoon in the pub. As a request he played me one of my favourite tracks - 'Bustin' Loose' by Chuck Brown & The Soul Searchers. It was a great way to finish the day off.

The next morning, bright eyed and bushy tailed, we made our way back over that charming Foundry Bridge and caught the train to Great Yarmouth. From there we were to take the X1 bus service down to Hopton. The main bus station in Great Yarmouth is not the most salubrious and I cannot envisage a time when it would ever win a 'Bus Station of the Year' award, if there is such a thing. Yes, it is covered and yes, it is conveniently situated in the centre of town.

But my goodness, whoever designed it must have been having a bad day. Backing on to the Market Gates shopping centre, it is predominantly dank, dark and gloomy. The locals appear overly eager to contribute to the bleakness with several discarded empty cans of strong cider to be found rattling about in the channelled draught, accompanied by the previous evening's kebab cartons that had been thoughtlessly littered on to the concrete. It was grimness personified but we only had a short time to wait for our bus and thankfully wouldn't need to be there for very long.

You'll be surprised to learn that some people are actually drawn to the desolation and for some mystifying reason choose to be there, like a kamikaze moth heading for a flame. A chap who was sat on a bench in the stand adjacent to ours was fastidiously rolling a cigarette/joint. A couple of buses stopped in front of him with passengers disembarking and embarking but he wasn't in the least bit interested, not even raising his head from his very important task. After a while he forcefully threw the finished article down onto the floor and exclaimed, to no one other than himself, "You fucking IDIOT. You do this every fucking TIME. What the FUCK is wrong with you?" I could only guess that his tobacco/weed rolling skills had deserted him and that he wasn't berating himself for failing to get on either of those buses. As other people queuing around me didn't bat an eyelid to this performance, I assumed it to be a common occurrence. The act felt apt considering its surroundings.

The X1 hissed to a halt and I began to feel the pulses of excitement rush through my body. This was it...we were on our way to the starting line at Hopton! The X1 is often referred to as being 'possibly Britain's longest bus journey' at 120 miles between first pick-ups at Peterborough and final drop-offs at Lowestoft. On our section this morning, we would be covering approximately 6 miles that would take half an hour.

As we snaked our way through the early morning Gorleston traffic I glanced out of the window, just in the nick of time, to see a blue plaque that was attached to an unassuming red-brick wall, incongruously above a grey and a green wheelie bin and just below a couple of satellite dishes. I must confess, I do love a blue plaque. Installed on publicly visible locations they commemorate either a famous person who lived or worked in that building (or site) or an important event that occurred within. This one was dedicated to Dr Kenneth Hamilton-Deane (1898-1993) who had practiced there ('Site of Surbiton Lodge') for a staggering 62 years between 1923 and 1985, thus making him 'The country's longest serving general practitioner'. Isn't that phenomenal? A whopping 62 years as a GP. How many patients had he seen? How many viruses had he come across? How different had the world changed around him in that time? He'd seen numerous fashion trends, hairstyles and he'd worked through World War II. He'd even been diagnosing patient's illnesses as long back as when Ipswich Town had last won a half-decent trophy and that is a very long time ago indeed, let me tell you.

The bus chugged into Hopton where we got off just down the road from the White Hart pub. On first impressions it appeared to be a sleepy little settlement nestled on the Norfolk/Suffolk border - a quiet and unassuming tourist resort. There were no big wheels, helter-skelters or piers to be seen here. Head down towards the sea and it's a different kettle of fish. The village's claim to fame is that it is home to Potters Resorts (founded in 1920) which is the UK's only All-Inclusive holiday resort. They employ nearly 600 permanent staff making them, by far, the largest private sector employer in the area. Every January they play host to the World Indoor Bowls Championships where players, spectators and the BBC decamp in the village for what is regarded as the biggest event in the bowls calendar. Early on an

October Monday morning it was difficult for me to envisage the amount of activity that this tournament must attract.

Walking down the secluded and tree-lined Beach Road to reach the official start/finish point of the Norfolk Coast Path, we were joined by a lady cyclist who informed us that she was going for her daily swim in the sea, if conditions were suitable. The last time I'd been to Hopton (20 years previously) there had been old wooden groynes optimistically protecting the coastline, but she told us these had recently been replaced by strategically placed rock-berms. 'What's a rock-berm Neil', I hear you ask. Well thanks for enquiring. They are structures made of large rocks/boulders (between 10 and 15 tonnes in weight) that are placed along the shoreline to protect against erosion caused by waves and tides. The unevenness of the rocks allow water to flow around them, causing the waves to release energy. The voids between the boulders play just as important a role as the rocks themselves as they help to further absorb the sea's might. The berms therefore play a crucial role in helping to safeguard coastal areas, buying them some much needed time in their efforts to ensure the long-term resilience of these sensitive shorelines.

The lady was in luck. There was hardly a wisp of wind as the gentle morning sun twinkled down onto the calm waves. With the rocks stretching out into the water like all-embracing arms the sea was like a millpond. "Looks like you're going to have a great swim" we enthused, nodding towards the sea as she carefully placed her bike down. "Hope you enjoy your walk" she replied, before adding "It looks like it's the golf course for you unless you fancy getting your feet wet too" while pointing back down the coast in the direction we were taking. "The tide's in."

The alternative route brought us out in an arc through a housing estate and onto an enjoyable promenade walk along the cliff top before sloping down into Gorleston with its wide and curving sandy beach. Fronted by brightly coloured flower boxes the lower esplanade and its crescent of attractive seaside shops looked exquisite. 'Family fun for everyone' was to be found here amongst the amusement arcade, chippy, ice cream parlour, café, restaurant and 'Yacht Shop'. To the naked eye the town looked to be in 'good nick', an observation that was only enhanced as we caught site of the splendid Pavilion Theatre. This Edwardian building, located close to the mouth of the River Yare, was designed by a borough engineer named JW Cockrill and built in 1898. Now under the controls of the Gorleston Pavilion Trust, the future looked secure for the next generation of theatregoers who would continue to be entertained by a comprehensive schedule of much-loved traditional productions as well as new and exciting shows that audiences had not yet seen.

Due to there being no crossing over the estuary at this point, the path headed back in land once more for the long stretch back towards the neighbouring seaside heavyweight that is Great Yarmouth. There were two types of Norfolk Coast Path signs along this part that we had not seen before; one being 'difficult to spot' stickers that were fixed onto the back of lamp posts, the other being metal waymarkers that had, without exception, been vandalised by local morons so that they were facing any way other than where they should have been. The mind boggles doesn't it? I wonder what the thought process is (if there is one) for these incredibly stupid people? I wonder if it's something along the lines of Moron #1 saying "Hey bro. Let's have a great night out by bending some path signs." Moron #2 replies "Yeah dude. Great idea…and when we've finished that we'll go to Yarmouth bus station and lob some empty cider cans and kebab containers onto the floor." Moron #1 "Sounds banging bro. Let's go." Is that how it gets underway? I've no idea and probably never will have but what I do know is that when they've finished I hope they go and fuck themselves.

As this is the 21st century we don't necessarily

need the waymarkers to traverse our way around suburban areas and through town centres, although it is always helpful to have them available. As a rule, we now just get our mobiles out and utilise the most powerful search engine in the world to find our way. Admittedly, while in the process, we blindly bump into fellow pedestrians, experience some hairy moments on zebra crossings and have the odd head-on altercation with a traffic sign but generally we find our way don't we. This is how the adorable Alisha and I navigated our way out of Gorleston, along Southtown Road, over the river and into Hall Quay before heading through the buzz of Great Yarmouth town centre and back to the coast. The highlights of this part of the walk were us seeing:

The Old Lighthouse Tower in Gorleston – 69ft high, made of red brick and built in 1878.

Herring Bridge (Great Yarmouth's third river crossing) – still under construction when we passed-by but fully-opened to road traffic in February 2024.

Star Hotel – located on Hall Quay, wonderful black and white façade featuring an intricate timber, flint and herringbone brick design. Closed in March 2020. I would have liked to have gone in for a pint or two in its heyday.

…and finally, the Poundstretcher store on Regent Road, where 'every penny counts'. Distinctive window display bearing clear details of many 'star deals', the building is predominantly decorated in a fetching red hue.

You've probably twigged I'm only kidding with the last one. I thought I'd include it as there is a bus shelter situated directly outside...and in said bus shelter was to be found our cigarette/joint rolling acquaintance from earlier in the day! I can report that, although he had exchanged venues, he was still struggling to master the task at hand and was continuing to profoundly eff and jeff as he went about his business.

On reaching Britannia Pier we headed north along the wide walkway, the sea being a fair way-off over the sand and away in the distance to our right. A visitor centre was passed, followed by well-maintained bowling greens, several thriving cafes, the sparkling Venetian Waterways (constructed in 1926 by men of the local parish in a project designed to boost post-war employment and tourism) and a boating lake. We then joined North Drive to avoid a potentially harrowing slog over the dunes and after a while encountered a forlorn looking, neglected and derelict pub building surrounded by ugly metal security barriers that were embedded in a variety of weeds. Its name was the Iron Duke.

Designed by esteemed architect Arthur William

'Billy' Ecclestone, construction began on this rare and unusually grand Art-Deco style hostelry in the late 1930s. Work was soon halted due to the outbreak of World War II although, even though the property was incomplete, the pub received its first licence in 1940 to serve soldiers who were manning anti-aircraft guns on the facing North Denes dunes. Designated as a flagship inn for local brewery Lacons, building was finally completed in 1948. Trading for the best part of 60 years, it was closed and boarded up by 2008.

I've already mentioned, earlier in this chapter, that I would have liked to have gone into the Star Hotel when it was still trading but only in a slightly wistful 'wouldn't have minded going in there for a pint or two' manner. But faced with the once stunning edifice of the Iron Duke, and with a severe (and befuddling) feeling of nostalgia, I hankered to go inside to a time when it was in its prime, when it was thriving with customers, when it would have been a 'go to' venue for many. Furthermore, I wanted to give it a big old proverbial hug as though I had come across a long-lost friend who had fallen on hard times.

Funny thing nostalgia isn't it, and I don't mean funny in a 'Ha-ha! It ain't wot it used to be' sort of way. I've never been prone to homesickness for example, particularly for somewhere I'd never been before. School/workplace reunions have never been my thing and I would not deem it to be an ideal use of my time to take part in a battle re-enactment or a 1940s weekend, although if that is your passion then 'hats-off' to you. I found it puzzling that I had an urge to want to travel back in time to a place I'd never been before, to a place I had never known.

I needed to know more about its past and what the future held. I was fortunate to get in touch with Caroline Jones, spokesperson for 'Friends of the Iron Duke', a group of mainly local people dedicated to the protection and restoration of this wonderful venue. She's passionate, a force of nature and a breath of fresh air all rolled into one. She told me that since formation, in what has been a huge overall community effort, the group have (amongst a myriad of achievements):

- Saved the pub from demolition in 2017
- Got it Grade II listed by Historic England, also in 2017
- Been the chief and widely acknowledged contact point for any enquiries
- Maintained overall focus on development
- Policed the building for 7 years

Regarding the future, and in order to obtain a semblance of balance to my research, I thought it responsible of me to contact Great Yarmouth Preservation Trust (GYPT) who are the current owners of the building. I can report that I tried on several occasions but never received a single reply from them. It was therefore left for Caroline to kindly fill in the gaps.

She told me the pub is to become a multi-use destination site featuring a chop-house restaurant, a bar featuring local ales (with the new incarnation of Lacons Brewery on board to provide the beers), holiday lets and possibly an Escape Room experience in the large basement. The operators will be the Norfolk restaurant chain, Zak's. All this is dependent on GYPT securing the next level of funding from the National Lottery Heritage Fund to cover the interior renovations. If the application is successful, the doors could be open as soon as Winter 2025. I would like to think I'll be one of the first persons through them - and I'll be buying Caroline a pint for her efforts.

One last thing about nostalgia before I move on. My English Language teacher at senior school once told the class a 'joke'. Do you want me to tell you it? Good. Here we go.

Q: Why is nostalgia like grammar?

A: Because we find the present tense and the past perfect.

I know, I know - 'Ba-Dum-Tissssssss', followed by a few tumbleweeds...

Leaving the Iron Duke, the humongous caravan parks of this part of Great Yarmouth and the firm-footed pavements behind, we trudged along the soft sanded beach and dunes before reaching Caister lifeboat station. Home to the first of only two independent UK offshore lifeboats, this hardy group of volunteers are affiliated to the National Independent Lifeboat Association (NILA), a new charity that was launched in 2022 to promote and support independent lifeboats across the UK (and not affiliated with the Royal National Lifeboat Institution (RNLI)). Having a rich history of saving lives at sea since 1791, they provide safety and rescue services to the countless vessels, crews and beach visitors to this area of the East Coast.

Over 120 years ago in November 1901, on a stormy night and in heavy seas, tragedy struck when the station's Beauchamp lifeboat capsized close to the beach trapping several members underneath of whom nine were killed. This catastrophe is still acknowledged as one of the most notably tragic in lifeboat history. At the subsequent inquiry former coxswain James Haylett was called as a witness. It was suggested to him that the lifeboat was returning having failed to complete the rescue and that the crew had given up in their rescue attempts. He replied 'No, they never give up. Coming back is against the rules'. This response has widely been interpreted as 'Caister men never turn back', a phrase that still captures the public's imagination to this day and has become the station's motto. A marble memorial stands in Caister cemetery as a fitting and moving tribute to the bravery of the perished crew. Featuring a broken mast, an anchor, laurel wreathes and a lifebuoy, it is also a poignant reminder of the sacrifices made by valiant members from a local community.

Intriguingly, a short stroll further along the beach from the lifeboat station, there's a different type of memorial in the form of a public house. Named the 'Never Turn Back' it is another designed by AW Ecclestone in his customary Art-Deco/Streamline-Moderne style. Built during 1956 it was officially opened on 19th June 1957 by Patrick Howarth who was the public secretary of the RNLI. It's nowhere near as grand, or as pleasing to the eye, as the Iron Duke – on first impressions it looks as though an old cricket scoreboard is flanked on either side by two vintage holiday camp chalets – and yet it still exudes a certain amount of charisma in its own quirky way. The only pub in England bearing this name, it achieved a Grade II listing in May 2018.

Leesh and I sensibly decided not to stop for a quick

drink, agreeing to carry on for an hour or so until we were closer to our accommodation for the evening. I'd initially booked a place on the California Sands Chalet Park but, shortly before our trip commenced, I'd received an urgent message from the owner to say that she'd unfortunately have to cancel due to a very important family matter. I went on the chalet owners Facebook group to see if anyone else had a vacancy at such short notice and, to my delight, received a message from a diamond of a lady called Carol Pennycook who offered us one of her three chalets for free! She'd noted that we were raising money for a charity (Cavell Nurses' Trust, if you're asking) and made the generous offer as she 'opens her doors for free' four times a year for partakers of such events. How fantastic is that!

My pace had slowed down considerably since leaving the firm-footed terrain experienced earlier in the day. Pleasingly, no injuries had re-surfaced but my legs were aching somewhat, possibly attributed to the recent virus that had afflicted me. I lumbered on along the beach at the side of my very understanding and patient daughter until, just after passing the Haven Holiday Park, my speed miraculously increased in tandem with heightened anticipation as we headed back inland towards the Centurion pub on Ormesby Road.

A 1960's build, it's a family-run establishment geared up mainly for holiday trade. Bi-fold doors are a recently installed feature, opening out onto a nicely sized beer garden and children's play area at the front of the property. A 'good selection of drinks' is advertised but, as I hurtled expectantly towards the bar, I was to find two out of the three hand pulls not in use with just the ominously named Doom Bar from Sharp's Brewery available on cask. I've read on the brewery's website that it 'is a perfectly balanced beer combining subtle yet complex flavours. This creates an amber ale which is both satisfying and deliciously moreish'. My palate tends to interpret this description into 'a nose of stagnant water with the added flavour of gravy granules suggesting a finish of garden compost'. I'm obviously missing something as the beer is apparently the UK's best-selling cask and bottled ale (oh, and for the record, it is named after the treacherous Doom Bar sandbank that lies at the mouth of the Camel Estuary at Rock in Cornwall).

I gave this beer a swerve and, after running my eyes up and down the line-up of lager/cider options, plumped for a pint of (whisper it quietly) Coors Light, and very refreshing it was too. There's a really good food menu at the pub, particularly if you're hell-bent on devouring a heap of carbohydrates like Leesh and I were, incorporating:

- tempting 'snacks & sides' offerings of chips, cheesy chips, spicy wedges, cod goujons and onion rings
- appealing options 'from the grill' such as steak or chicken fillet burger (add cheese, cheese and bacon, beef chilli or prawns)
- and inviting 'classics' like cod & chips, all day breakfast and beef lasagne & chips

I was blumming ravenous, salivating involuntary and seriously contemplating making the biggest food order ever known to mankind as I approached the bar again, menu expectantly in hand, as the addictive and alluring aroma of recently cooked sustenance wafted out from the kitchen.

Barperson: "Oh I'm ever so sorry. We've finished doing food now for the afternoon. We do have bar snacks though…crisps, nuts…"

Me: "Fair enough. I'll have seventeen bags of cheese and onion crisps please."

Not really…I ordered ten bags. Maybe.

Still famished, the adorable Alisha and I made tracks for the 'Grange Smokehouse Bar & Grill' which was roughly on the route to our chalet. The wind had increased and the rain began to fall as we arrived 15 minutes before opening time. Creating a great first impression, a lady came outside to rescue us from the downpour, kindly ushering us inside to take a seat within the dry and warm interior.

A renowned southern style American diner, the 'Smokehouse' opened in September 2018 and is set in extensive and well-maintained grounds that incorporate a campsite. Inside, you can tell that the owners have given a lot of time, thought and effort to the décor, all adding to the overall ambience and customer experience. There's Route 66 petrol pumps, a jukebox, Betty Boo 'just doin' the do' and a life-size model of Elvis Presley keeping watch outside the Gents, where there will no doubt be (ahem) a 'whole lot-ta shakin' goin' on'. Thankyouverymuch.

The staff are super attentive, helpful and know both the food and drinks menus like the backs of their hands, gently giving advice if you're unsure what to order. I was struggling (for the second time of the day) to find something that I fancied to drink and was nudged in the direction of Woodforde's Wherry on keg – I'd never seen it in that guise before and very nice it was too.

The food was excellent as well. The meal portions were of a very generous size with little requirement to ask for the host of sides I anticipated I'd need to bulk up the order. There was a chap on the next table who apparently hadn't learned from a previous experience…

He'd ordered 'THE TRIPLE BYPASS' burger. The clue to the size of the meal is perhaps in the name. The bumf went as follows: *'Our belly buster! Five patties stacked high with pulled pork, pulled chicken, brisket, cheese & onion rings. Over 35oz of meat heaven!'* All burgers came with *'House Fries, Salad Garnish, House Slaw & Pickles'*. Now, you can think of me as being extremely perceptive, but I'm telling you this – that little lot would take some time and effort to finish off even for the most committed of gorgers.

Encircled by an embarrassment of huge plates heaped with grilled animal flesh of different sorts, beads of sweat began to fall down his brow before he'd even attempted to pick up his knife. I immediately wondered if the idiomatic expression 'he'd bitten off more than he could chew' had been coined specifically for this one moment in his life. He blew out of his mouth in apprehension, like a hesitant whale on reaching the water's surface, and began his ordeal.

His wife looked at him and observed "I don't know why the fuck you've ordered that. You must be mad. Last time you had it you had to leave it as you felt really ill." The chap didn't respond.

Leesh and I began to watch in earnest, as did other diners. Bar and waiting-on staff became alert to that particular table with kitchen operatives also creeping into the restaurant for a peek. The word had got around. I also think I may have noticed a bus full of spectators from Lessingham who'd come through the doors especially to see what was occurring. This was spectator sport at its finest.

He started off at a fair old canter but it wasn't long before he needed a rest, carefully and systematically wiping his hands on a flimsy serviette. Was he having a breather, buying some time? Was he going to be able to continue?

His wife looked at him and observed "You're struggling already aren't you. I can tell. There's no way you're going to finish that. Your eyes are bigger than your belly. I bet you're feeling ill aren't you." The chap didn't respond.

He commenced his second attempt. He was 'giving it a go' but there were still mounds of food for him to get through. The Lessingham posse were beginning to take bets – he'd gone out from an initial 2/1 to tens. It wasn't looking good as he virtually ground to a halt. People began to shake their heads in disappointment, exchanging knowing looks, ripping up their betting slips. He'd obviously had enough and was refusing to finish.

Painstakingly wiping his hands again, he finally admitted to his wife "I feel really ill" before emitting a monumental belch that was probably heard out on the

Scroby Sands Wind Farm. He then got up from his table and began to gradually walk away, leaving his partner to finish her meal ...and pay the tab.

"Tosser" she said.

Day 6 miles walked: 14.97 / Total miles walked: 69.79

SCRATBY TO HAPPISBURGH

We had no time to linger in Carol's lovely chalet as we prepared ourselves for another session of walking along the coast path. Our destination for the day was to be the charming and historic village of Happisburgh, where it will come as no surprise when I tell you that it is pronounced 'Haze-Bruh' and not 'Happ-Is-Berg' as you'd may assume.

With rucksacks duly repacked we eagerly made our way along Rottenstone Lane and around the corner onto Beach Road, to the remarkably well-stocked Scratby Bakery for breakfast (2 large sausage rolls for me, bacon roll and millionaire brownie for Leeshy). Doubling back on ourselves, we then rejoined the street that passes by the California Tavern and walked down the steps to the seashore.

For those of you who are familiar with the California/Scratby area, you may be wondering why we didn't take the first set of access steps down after visiting the bakery, which are next to the car park/public toilets. Well, I wanted to have a close-up look, from the beach, at the cliff-top properties along this specific stretch where it's not uncommon to see panels of fencing or sides of a shed draping down from ever-diminishing gardens towards the sand. This is not the likes of what we are used to seeing adjacent to railway tracks when we are on a train journey, where unloved and unrequired pieces of garden furniture have been heaved onto the embankment, and out of the way, in a mindless 'out of sight/out of mind/not my problem anymore' tactic. I'm talking about where items are dangling their own involuntary way down when crumbling land has suddenly fallen away, after extreme tidal surges in tandem with equally powerful winds. We were now entering the stretch of East Anglian shoreline that is arguably the most vulnerable to the devastating consequences of coastal erosion...

I've briefly touched on the topic before, such as when I mentioned the enforced meandering around the caravan parks of the 'Runtons', and out onto the pavement alongside the A149, due to the official path having deteriorated sufficiently to warrant a detour. As this area continues to cop a proper old bashing, courtesy of the brutally relentless North Sea, I will now be writing about it in greater detail, starting off with a few facts and figures that'll make you think.

The narrative of climate change and rising sea levels taking their toll on the landscape is not a new one. We know that over 300 settlements in the North Sea Basin have been lost in the last 900 years. Harrowingly, this never-ending and harmful threat looms over these coastal communities every single day, with the 'Shoreline Management Plan' predicting that by the year 2105 (and specifically for the immediate area we were currently walking along):

- **70 AND 130 SEAFRONT PROPERTIES WILL BE LOST BETWEEN CAISTER ON SEA AND CALIFORNIA**
- **55 AND 150 SEAFRONT PROPERTIES WILL BE LOST BETWEEN SCRATBY AND NEWPORT**

These are dreadful figures, aren't they? I was also shocked to learn that if you have a property that is threatened by coastal erosion it loses all value, becomes impossible to insure and you end up homeless, losing everything.

On the approach to Hemsby Beach, running alongside the Newport area, can be found a hideously defenceless area called The Marrams. It is an 'estate' of idiosyncratic, non-standard constructions of various shapes and sizes that can be described as huts, chalets or bungalows. Some have already perished, others have been dismantled or demolished before falling into the sea, while it was clear to observe as we walked through, that the remaining properties are facing hugely significant and most probably insurmountable challenges in the very near future. To exacerbate the issue, access roads have collapsed leaving vehicles stranded with nowhere to go, while the water supply can often be cut off after pipes have been ripped out in the resultant carnage. It is impossible not to get an all-encompassing feeling that these people have been abandoned.

Each coastal area faces its own unique challenges that are intrinsically linked to local conditions, available resources and government/community cooperation. There is no one magical 'fix-all' solution, plus, it is often the case that a specific type of defence structure implemented further up the coast can result in 'knock-on' problems being encountered elsewhere. It is also worth bearing in mind that whatever the type of protection that's constructed will not have the slightest bit of impact on the rising and subsequent might of the sea. Managing coastal erosion can be classed by heartless casual observers as being 'eye wateringly expensive' and yet, if it's your home that's at threat, it has got to be worth the cost. The cynical bottom line is that there is only a limited amount of money available meaning some areas (towns and larger settlements) will hit the jackpot and continue to be protected while other impoverished and smaller ones sadly will not. What is crucially needed is unblinking foresight and a thoroughly comprehensive long-term action plan, neither of which appear to be the strongest attributes of squabbling political parties and respective local authorities.

Approximately a mile away from The Marrams, just off the centre of Hemsby Village, lies the 12th century church of St. Mary the Virgin. Perhaps the congregation may want to pray that this close-knit community receives the urgent assistance it desperately requires, with their properties miraculously spared from the devastating effects of the cruel elements.

Hemsby itself is split into two distinct sections; one being an attractive little village that straddles the B1159 (a 32 mile stretch of road serving the coastal communities between Cromer and Caister on Sea) and the other being a compact and lively seaside resort that is tucked away down Beach Road.

As we arrived the beach was temporarily cut off due to a landslip, the toilets were out of action and the lifeboat was unable to launch as the temporary slipway had been wiped away. Still, none of this seemed to perturb a lively throng of loyal visitors who unwaveringly went about their business; some were enthusiastically shovelling money into the slots, others patiently waited for their numbers to be called out at bingo while the hard-core tea drinkers dreamily gazed into space with their prized brew on the table in front of them. It was uplifting to see Hemsby thriving with tourism – a symbolic 'poke in the eye' on the savage face of climate crisis.

Leesh and I plodded on, now heading towards Winterton along a grassy expanse of land known as 'The Valley', a rather pleasant and secluded area consisting of low-lying scrub and random sandy craters that were flanked by banks of various types of coarse vegetation. It resembled the narrowest and least maintained golf course of all time consisting of threadbare fairways, bunkers containing wildly sprouting marram grass and rutted greens where there wasn't a hole or flag to be seen. Maybe I was having visions; maybe I needed another sausage roll, who knows. I contented myself with the thought that at least our walk wasn't being spoiled by having to play eighteen holes of golf, as many weekly walks are for a whole host of amateurs.

We all know someone like that don't we, who every Sunday come rain or shine, obsessively hauls their clubs out of the shed and into the back of the estate car for yet another frustrating and infuriating round of hacking, swishing, six-putting and cussing their way around their local course.

There's a chap who comes into my local pub (the award-winning Rose & Crown, Brampton, Chesterfield) who fits this description to a (ahem) tee. After a typical round of golf, I often hear him babbling on about managing a par on the 'challenging' sixth hole. Everyone in earshot knows he's likely to be bullshitting and has probably kept nudging his ball further forward with his toe-end when he thinks no one is looking, while also 'forgetfully' not adding a stroke on here and there. He's not a bad soul though and recently found the need to text me with a crucial issue.

Golfer: *Mate. I know I dont usually Txt u about these things but I cud really do wi some advice*

Me: *Go on then mate. Go for it…*

Golfer: *wELL I recon my missus could be cheating on me. All the signs are there. She's out wi her mates all the* time, gets in late that sort of thing. But when I ask her wot shes bin UP to and where shes bin she just clams up

Me: *OOOOF doesn't sound good that mate…*

Golfer: *Tell me about it. anyway ive bin trying to stay awake the last few times shes bin out so I can look out for her comin in and see who shes wi but I keep nodding off*

Me: *Riiiiiiiiiiitteeee…*

Golfer: *Anyways last night i made a right effort to check up on her. i went into shed and left door slightly open so I could get a good view*

Me: *Riiiiiiiiiiitteeee…*

Golfer: *well, I hid behind my bag of golf clubs so she couldn't spot me and as she came into view, and as i crouched behind my clubs, I spotted summat that really really really disturbed me*

Me: *OMG…wot was it???!!!*

Golfer: *well I don't know how to tell u this but I noticed that the graphite shaft on my driver appeared to have a hairline crack right at the side of the club head! so wot I wanna know is dya recon this is summat I can fix myself or shall i take it back to the golf shop I brought if from??? Cheers*

You'll be impressed to note that I advised him to ask his wife to drop it off at the shop while she was on her way out with her 'mates'. I know, I know, I'm a genius…

As I physically wandered along the alternate,

fantasy 'golf course' my mind continued to roam mentally. It was one of those days. At one stage I thought I'd been transported into another distant and strange land – and no, I don't mean Suffolk. I'm talking about another continent. 'Why's that then Neil', I hear you ask. Well, let me explain. As I looked over to my left, peering over a hedge appeared to be primitive-looking circular mud huts adorned with grassed roofs. What the heck were they doing in Winterton? Was I walking through the properties of a reclusive community of people from faraway who all share the same culture and dialect, linked by social, economic, religious and blood ties…and happened to settle in Norfolk?

I'll put your mind at rest. It is the site of a unique self-catering holiday park. These colourful African-style cottages, with their characteristic thatched roofs, were inspired by the rondavels of Hermanus Bay in South Africa and are part of the history of this complex that was initially the site of a country home.

The home became an upmarket hotel after having been acquired by an ex-RAF pilot named Ken Temple. He'd spent time living in Africa and it was he who had the iconic roundhouses built to accommodate extra guests. The hotel was of the exclusive type and was used to hosting high profile guests such as Honor Blackman and Richard Burton – the latter alleged to have been happy to 'chat up' a local girl when attending a glittering event there.

Run by the Denton family for nigh on the last fifty years, innovation has proved key in successfully negotiating the holiday industry's notorious peaks and troughs. It has been a base for a popular cellar disco as well as being a leading UK venue for country and western music.

Looking out over the dunes, the complex looks ideally situated for people who need a base for exploring the coastline, its remote sandy beaches and the areas host of nature reserves. It is those cheery-looking roundhouses that catch the eye and give this place a distinction over comparable organisations.

From Winterton we were now entering a stage of the coast path that, in its own way, was as wild, empty and beautiful as the salt marshes experienced in the first half of the walk. Towards Horsey no one was encountered, not even an intrepid seal spotter, which rather surprised me. This naturally raw and remote area consisting of flat beaches, shallow waters and high dunes is an ideal location for the aquatic mammals to give birth on.

As proof of just how many people can descend here at certain times of the year, a group of volunteer wardens called the Friends of Horsey Seals (FoHS) 'police' the location by offering visitors designated viewing areas that are a safe stretch away, leaving the seals in relative peace.

Most sightseers are respectful and use a common-sense approach by naturally maintaining a reasonable distance. Unfortunately, there are imbeciles amongst them who have no qualms with behaving irrationally. I've seen photos where groups of morons are milling around the wild seals in the manner that they'd gormlessly wander around a collection of domesticated, docile animals at a local petting zoo on a Sunday morning. What are they expecting to happen? For the seals to start purring in appreciation of their presence, adoringly wrapping their flippers around ankles in a show of adoration? These are the type of people who expect to see the seals come out of the sea balancing a fucking beach ball on their nose while riding a unicycle and singing 'Come on Eileen'...and if they don't, they give the seals a shit review on Tripadvisor.

There are reports aplenty detailing other acts of stupidity such as:

- A man 'taunting' a pregnant seal
- Dog attacks after owners have let them off their leads ('It's OK...he/she won't hurt you, he/she only wants to play'. We've all heard this haven't we?)

- Individuals chasing and deliberately scaring seals
- People attempting selfies

Seriously.

Absolute cretins aren't they. Then again, you may have observed warning notices on certain items that you have recently purchased, warning notices that for many would seem to be superfluous. Let's have a look at a few:

- On a laser printer cartridge – DO NOT EAT TONER
- On a dishwasher – DO NOT ALLOW CHILDREN TO PLAY IN THE DISHWASHER
- On a car battery – DO NOT DRINK THE CONTENTS OF THE BATTERY
- On a pram – REMOVE CHILD BEFORE FOLDING

Seriously.

These are specifically directed at the idiots mentioned above; the taunters, the inconsiderate dog owners, the chasers, the scarers and the selfie hunters. Sadly, while this is all going on, the long-term survival of the seals is being seriously impacted.

But today, there wasn't a soul to be seen. The seals could temporarily breathe a sigh of relief.

Endless blue skies and glittering sea views were a mesmerising back drop as we continued in a north-westerly direction along the top of the dunes. It felt as though we were looking down with a privileged view, of not only this little section of Norfolk but of the whole world. This altered abruptly as we headed inland, before eventually sidling down a narrow alley wedged between two garden fences that made us feel like we could be trespassing. We were now entering the small community of Sea Palling.

This compact resort village is another that is historically no stranger to the devastating effects of flooding and the subsequent destruction caused by those ever-powerful waves. For the time-being it does appear that the residents can relax as significant defences have recently been implemented just off the shoreline in the form of nine artificial reefs. Timber and steel groynes had reached the end of their usefulness and, in a major operation, been replaced by 24,000 tonnes of rock (individually weighing between 10-15 tonnes each, like the ones we saw in Hopton) transported by barge from Norway. In a complex manoeuvre that took around 6 weeks to complete, the main barge was anchored offshore while a smaller barge transferred the rocks to the beach at high tide in manageable loads of 1200 tonnes. At low tide, the rocks were picked up by excavators and placed into the required position. Strategically sited parallel to the coast, this flood defence scheme is a fascinating example of what can be achieved in coastal engineering.

The adorable Alisha and I walked along the spacious and serene beach, the clear waters lapping lightly onto the golden sands. As I began to flag, it looked like an ideal spot for a refreshing and rejuvenating dip...but there was no time to dally here. I was getting ready for a pint and we still had another four miles to ramble before reaching the revered Hill House pub in 'Haze-Bruh'. Leesh must have been having similar thoughts as she glanced at me, before nodding her head up the coast. "Come on big lad. Get them feet moving. Not long to go now!"

As well as those nine artificial reefs, North Gap, Eccles on Sea and Cart Gap came and went before we were soon heading on to the cliff tops with the enchanting Happisburgh lighthouse in the near distance to our left. It is the only independently run light in Great Britain and proudly remains the oldest working one in East Anglia. Built in 1790 it was originally one of a pair (the 'low light' stood 20ft lower and was discontinued in 1883), the tower being 85ft tall with the lantern 134ft above sea level. Both formed leading lights marking a safe passage around the southern end of the nearby treacherous sandbank.

I was taking in the view of this 'easy on the eye' historic edifice, painted white with three famously distinctive candy-cane red bands, when I heard Leesh mutter "Dad, have a look at this. I think there may be a wedding taking place on the beach. There's a group of people milling around and they're all dressed in red." I took little notice, preferring to ogle at the structure erected to save shipping along this section of the North Sea – and don't you find it almost dream-like when you have only ever viewed a famous landmark in photographs on all sorts of brochures, postcards and guides and then, as if by magic, it appears in front of you in all its glory just a few yards away?

As two uncoordinated and chilling clangs of a bell sounded, Leesh attempted to alert me again. "Dad, I really think you should have a look at this" and as I peered down onto the beach I saw the weirdest sight.

The 'clangs' had sounded from the 'Time & Tide Bell', a large structure permanently secured onto the sands and designed to be rung by the waves at high tide to produce a varying and gentle musical pattern. But it wasn't the sea that had created the sounds that I'd heard. For, as I looked in the general direction of where the noise had emanated from, and to my total disbelief, I saw eight people. All had ghostly white-painted faces (at first I thought they were Pierrot clown masks), all were wearing scarlet robes and all were dramatically draped around the bell. It had been struck twice to signify the commencement of what appeared to be some form of pagan ritual and, for the third time in what was fast becoming the most peculiar of days, I wondered if I was hallucinating.

We watched captivated, unable to take our eyes off the mysterious and red-attired figures as they continued to slowly circle around the bell, almost caressing it as they did so, like it was a mystical object releasing superior and tantalising powers that only they could sense and feel. This eerie spectacle continued until one of them struck it twice more, signalling the end of the sequence, before they all compliantly joined hands and very, very steadily began to walk away from Happisburgh along the sand, in a single line, in silence. To where, we did not know.

We looked at each other with eyes and mouths agape.

Me: "What...the...flipping..."

Daughter: "No...idea...dudey"

Me: "I need a beer"

Daughter: "Me too"

Ten minutes later (at 15:15) we keenly arrived at

the doors to the Hill House pub where I had booked in for the evening. As I was about to enter, massively gagging for a pint as you may imagine, a man and woman who were sat outside sharing a bottle of wine smugly informed us "Oh they closed fifteen minutes ago...and they don't re-open until 5."

FUCK!!!!!!! FUCK!!!!!!! FUUUUUUUCK!!!!!!!

Fortunately, landlady Sue Stockton had kindly left a note on the door requesting us to call her mobile on arrival, which I promptly did before I could succumb to the temptation of wanting to pour the liquid contents of the wine container over the self-satisfied couple's heads.

Sue kindly welcomed us to her beautiful Hill House pub, perceptively asked us what we would like to drink, then showed us to where we would be staying – a magnificent, bona-fide railway signal box. It had been built on the premises in 1901 as part of the planned, but never completed, expansion of the Great Eastern Railway that was to run from North Walsham through to Happisburgh, before heading south-easterly to Great Yarmouth. Sympathetically converted to eclectic self-contained accommodation with en suite, as we reached the top of the stairs it positively oozed with rustic charm, while a glimpse through the expansive window offered us wonderfully elevated and evocative views out to sea.

This was brilliant! There was also a witty 'warning' sign on the wall, light-heartedly taking the piss out of all the people who may be recreationally interested in trains and/or rail transport systems, such as me I guess. It read:

BEWARE

RAIL ENTHUSIASTS DISEASE

HIGHLY INFECTIOUS TO MALES OF ALL AGES

THE SYMPTONS: The sufferer becomes confused and bewildered when not near a railway. Will be observed wandering around with blank expression, muttering strangewords. Rapid rise in temperature at sight of a train. Behaviour then becomes erratic: much rushing about and waving of arms. Foaming at the mouth is not unusual. Is sometimes violent to non-believers. The Patient spends much time and money at book and magazine shops. Seems not to notice presence of "Normal" people.

THIS CONDITION IS NOT FATAL

THE TREATMENT: Patient must be kept well supplied with items of railway interest. Should be encouraged to go on steam tours and to open-days where he can meet other victims of the illness and exchange ideas with them. Friends and relations can aid recovery with free transport, free beer and meals. In case of emergency contact your nearest preservation society.

I'd like to take this opportunity to officially confirm that I'm principally interested in the offers of free transport, free beer and free meals and am publicly announcing the fact that I will now be enthusiastically pursuing family members and good mates in order to obtain these items. Many thanks, in anticipation.

The Hill House Inn has a deep and vibrant history, first appearing in records as far back as 1540. Three distinct Tudor cottages were knocked into one and, sometime between 1610 and 1630, this property began to brew and sell ale (remnants of the original brewery still exist on site).

Circa 1710, there is reference to the ale house being called the Windmill Inn, by now having developed into a notable coaching stop on the vital coast route between two of the country's busiest ports of the time, namely King's Lynn and Great Yarmouth. By the late 1790's the pub was attracting a broad clientele, ranging from illustrious patrons such as the poet William Cowper and his cousin the clergyman Dr John Johnson, to dubious local characters such as beach men and smugglers. Around this time, the pub was renamed the Hill House Inn, possibly in an attempt to reform its reputation, or maybe they just simply fancied a name change.

By the Edwardian era, the hostelry had acquired a desirable and respected standing in the community, enticing many distinguished guests as a result. One of these was none other than Sir Arthur Conan Doyle (1859-1930), the prolific writer who created the character (and our old pal, 'no shit') Sherlock Holmes. According to Cameron Self of the 'Literary Norfolk' website, the author visited the Hill House in 1903 while on a motoring holiday. During his stay he was asked to sign an autograph book and was intrigued to find a signature of the landlord's seven-year-old son, Gilbert Cubitt, consisting solely of 'pin men'. This inspired Conan Doyle to write the classic mystery tale *The Dancing Men* (now usually referred to as *The Adventure of The Dancing Men*) while at the pub.

In the story, Holmes and his faithful sidekick Doctor Watson, are called to Norfolk by a local squire Hilton Cubitt, to investigate a series of strange drawings that culminate in a shadowy death. The proficient sleuth solves the case by cracking a code which consists of little dancing figures, similar to those produced by young Gilbert Cubitt. As can be seen, Conan Doyle also took the surname 'Cubitt' from his visit. Another local link is that the squire lives in the fictional Ridling Thorpe Manor, this name almost certainly being a composite of local villages Ridlington and Edingthorpe. The villain in the story, an American called Abe Slaney, lodges at a farmhouse in nearby East Ruston, which is an actual village.

A blue plaque, unveiled in 2006, is proudly

attached to the front wall of the Hill House Inn, commemorating the author's stay there.

…and by the way, I wonder if there's any truth in the rumour that the phrase often attributed to Holmes, 'ALE-mentary, my dear Watson' was also coined in the pub?

As the clock struck '5' Leeshy and I zoomed out of the signal box 'like shit off a shovel', this railway idiom relating back to the heady days of steam when trains had a driver plus a fireman to load coal. I'll not go any deeper on this as I don't want to put you off your dinner. You what? You really want me to explain? Fair enough. You asked…

Well, every now and again, the fireman would find himself in dire need of answering a call of nature, specifically of the 'Number Two' category. In what must have been an intricate and precise operation, he would duly dump his load onto the coal shovel and then fling the proceeds of such action into the fire, pronto, due to the smell and hygiene conditions. Since the shovel had coal dust on it, the dollop did not stick and pleasingly flirted off at a rapid pace. Now here's where it gets interesting. That very same shovel would be cleaned (to what extent I'm not too sure) by utilising the outpouring of steam with the fireman, now much lighter and sprightlier, promptly cooking bacon and eggs on it.

I tend not to be of too squeamish a disposition but, I'm telling you this, if I'd have been the driver, breakfast would have been given a huge swerve. Bluuuurrrgghhhh...

On the bar, there was a healthy four beers for me to choose from: Lacons Encore (3.8% amber ale), Mr Winter's Peach Tea (4% pale ale), Hardys & Hansons Olde Trip (4.3% session bitter) and White Rose Brewery White Dragon (4.5% pale ale).

For food, we selected from the 'House Favourites' section of the menu, with Leesh choosing 'Scampi' while I had 'Ham & Eggs', both coming with 'Chips and Peas'. Now, for those of you whose culinary world consists of multi-sensory cooking, ambitious food combinations and scientific flavour encapsulation, then on the face of it, these two meals may not be classed as the most exciting that you will ever have seen. However, all I can say is that both were cooked to perfection, portions were bountiful and I wasn't out of pocket when paying the bill...and just for your information, we paired the Scampi with Lestrade lager and the Ham & Eggs with White Dragon. Pure brilliance!

Landlord Clive (Sue's husband) entered the scene, effortlessly networking his way around the assembly of happy and contented customers and had a kind and enthusiastic word for everyone. At one stage of his walkaround, he realised that punters who were sat at tables at the opposite ends of the pub, were from the same street of the same London borough, and thoughtfully introduced them to each other. He'd heard we were walking the coast path and was genuinely interested as he asked about our experiences so far, if we'd enjoyed our meal and what I thought to the quality of the ale.

It had been a memorable day in many ways and, at a sensible hour, we decided it was time to re-acquaint ourselves with that special signal box and 'hit the sheets' for a well-earned rest. I must confess, it would have been oh so easy to stay drinking and chatting in that wonderful establishment until the bell rang to signal closing time…

Bell??? Bell??? Did someone mention a bell??? You may have deliberated (as I had) who the red-clad, mysterious strangers were who clanked the 'Time & Tide Bell' earlier in the afternoon, and what their purpose had been. I can inform you they were members of the 'Red Rebel Brigade', their website explaining they '*are an international performance activist troupe dedicated to illuminating the global environmental crisis and supporting groups and organisations fighting to save humanity and all species from mass extinction*'. They were devised by Doug Francisco and Justine Squire from Bristol's Invisible Circus for the Extinction

Rebellion Spring uprising of April 2019 in London. The brigade's colour choice of red was an aesthetic and symbolic one, evoking strong emotive responses. The striking visual imagery is one of their great strengths, not only in the live urban environment but also in its capacity to grab attention and positioning with international media, helping push the content to prominent placement and reach more people. It captivates viewers online and in print as much as it does live and is a very powerful medium to carry the message.

Their powerfully enigmatic performance had made a big impression on Leesh and I. We could only hope that it had the same effect on the 'powers that be' in the East Coast's continuous fight against decimation. A stark and ever-present reminder of the plight of the region can be found in the form of a chilling warning that appears at the bottom of Clive and Sue Stockton's business information sheet:

The Hill House Inn is a Grade II listed building and will be preserved for as long as the sea does not engulf Happisburgh.

Day 7 miles walked: 16.04 / Total miles walked: 85.83

HAPPISBURGH
TO OVERSTRAND

On awakening in the splendid signal box, the early morning sun had already begun to filter in through the embroidered pair of white, net curtains strung along the panoramic window. I can confirm there was no need for me to flick the light switch on. This is worth mentioning as, the previous evening, a chap had told me that three trainspotters had stayed there the previous week and it had taken all of them to change a lightbulb; one to take the old one out and put the new one in, one to note down the serial numbers of both bulbs and one to hold his friends' anoraks. I knew he was fibbing as there must have been a fourth person in attendance who would have been responsible for carrying a thermos flask of tomato soup. You can't catch me out like that.

Sue was patiently waiting to serve our breakfasts as my daughter and I reacquainted ourselves with the interior of the Hill House Inn. This time we were sat in the charming little restaurant that was positively brimming with Sherlock Holmes memorabilia. Everywhere I looked there was something interesting that caught the eye. I then spotted what appeared to be a miniature replica of the local lighthouse.

"A-ha!" exclaimed the landlady. "There's a story behind that."

She told us there had been an earlier version that had resided just inside the pub's front porch. One day, an attentive neighbour alerted her to the fact that she'd seen someone nab the wooden model and sped off on his bike with it to apparent safety.

Sue was having none of this and swiftly began to give chase in the general direction indicated by her informant. This involved careering down local lanes and byways on her own two-wheeler, until the trail led onto the vast and remote expanse of dunes a few miles away. There she spied a tent where the accused had set up camp, surrounded by attractive planters and their relative plants that he'd also purloined from the outside of local B&Bs, cafes and private residences. She approached the thief's canvas shelter, incensed with his petty and devious misdemeanour.

"Oi you! Where's my lighthouse???!!!" she demanded.

"I've buried it somewhere over there" smirked the robber, pointing in the general direction of anywhere that was sandy in this part of Norfolk. "You're welcome to try and find it."

"You bastard!" exclaimed Sue. She knew she'd not got a hope of locating her prized ornament.

To the rescue came a couple of the pub's loyal customers (and regular visitors from the Midlands) who'd heard on the grapevine about the opportunistic theft. On their next trip east they brought Sue a model of a helter-skelter, similar in shape and size to the missing lighthouse, which she carefully and skilfully adapted to look like the original. It was this version that I was looking at now.

"I still miss the old one though" admitted Sue, forlornly.

We polished off our delicious, traditional brekkies and it was soon time to be on our way again, this time heading for Overstrand, on what was to be our last, strenuous and full day of walking. We'd really enjoyed our stay in 'Haze-Bruh' and were saying our grateful goodbyes when we received our final confirmation of the plight encountered in this part of the world and the ever-present threat to its existence. As Sue advised us of the quickest direction to get back on the official track, she glumly continued "You'll walk around the back of the pub and through what was a substantial caravan site before most of it recently fell into the sea...and don't forget, when that sea reaches our hedge, that's it. We'll have to cease trading. Our business is finished." She gave it twenty years, tops.

Looking out over the battered sea defences, as powerless as rotting matchsticks against the sea's power, I did wonder if I would ever get the chance to visit this charming place again. I really did hope so...

While rambling along the length of the Norfolk Coast Path you undoubtedly encounter a contrasting range of landscapes. There's sand spits and SHINGLE banks, saltmarshes and tidal creeks, soaring sandy cliffs and, in the next small village we arrived at, a low fortified shoreline. Walcott sits right on the edge of the coast with the B1159 running parallel to the beach, the only occasion we saw this on our journey. Staring straight into the face of the sea is a convenience store incorporating a post office, a couple of handily placed car parks, Kingfisher café, Kingfisher ice-cream parlour, Kingfisher fish bar and Kingfisher public conveniences. OK, I may have made the last one up.

Outside the latter of these premises are situated a couple of helpful information boards, one of which is titled 'Wandering through wild Walcott'. As with blue plaques, I must admit I do love a good information board. This one is not only interesting but thought provoking too. It explains *'Once our ancient ancestors stood here and looked out over vast open grassy plains and marshland, pierced by rivers, as far as the eye can see'* and instantly cajoles you into standing there and trying desperately to imagine this very view. It continues *'This land mass (known as Doggerland) connected us to modern day Europe and it is believed that what is now the Thames estuary originally flowed out through this landscape. Doggerland was swallowed by the sea some 8,000-10,000 years ago as a result of melting glaciers'.* A couple of pictures of the large Steppe mammoth (whose bones I mentioned were found in nearby West Runton in the early 1990's) are included to give the timeframe some perspective.

In a county that never ceases to amaze me with what has gone on in the past, I found this information astounding. How come I'd never paid much attention to the existence of Doggerland before, or the findings of long-extinct animal skeletons from thousands of years ago for that matter? I admit, if you do not reside in this part of East Anglia, it is a difficult place to keep track of, for both historical and current information. The national media does not appear to be in the slightest bit interested, preferring to concentrate on densely populated areas consisting of big cities that are rated more important due to economic reasons (and their subsequent financial significance to the UK overall) or conversely where there are more headline-grabbing occurrences of crime. It is a fact that a lot of 'Nelson's County' is empty and considered by many to be far away from the rest of the country, consequently positioning it peripherally in the nation's psyche when viewed alongside highly crowded metropolitan towns and cities. Even so, you'd think there would be a much deeper curiosity about, and better reporting of, Norfolk than there is. Let me give you an example…

In the summer of 1998, the shifting sands of the quiet and unassuming Holme beach (near Hunstanton) revealed something extraordinary. For preserved in the sand were the remains of a unique timber circle dating back over 4,000 years to the early Bronze Age. This stupefying structure became popularly known as 'Seahenge'. The circle was originally built on the saltmarsh away from the sea and specialists estimated it to have been built of timbers dating from the spring of 2049 BC. It would have been positioned in an area protected from the sea by dunes and mud flats. This swampy range created a layer of peat which slowly covered the timbers, protecting them from decay. The circle was 6.6m in diameter and comprised of 55 oak posts that surrounded a huge oak tree stump that had been buried upside-down with its roots uppermost. Originally standing up to 3m in height it is believed to have been constructed by the people of the local small farming communities. It remains an incredible monument to the skills and beliefs of our Bronze Age ancestors although, intriguingly, no one has ever been able to say, for definite, what its purpose was.

Whatever the reason, it would be a huge understatement to suggest that it must have been extremely important. Can you picture the scene where a bunch of old-school agriculturalists, sat around a campfire one night, stars twinkling in a clear dark sky, are contentedly getting hammered on some sort of poteen, when one of them says "Right then lads. I've got an idea. For a laugh, why don't we chop up an oak tree into loads of posts. We can then dig 55 holes, in a perfect circle, to put them in. As a showpiece, we'll dig up another fuck-off oak tree, then dig a bigger, mahoosive, fuck-off hole to bury it in, and because we're show-offs we'll put it in upside down. I reckon having the roots on top will be mega! Who's up for it?" It's not going to have happened is it. The 'henge' must have been created for a hugely significant intention but I guess we'll never know. As the farmer may even have concluded "...and to piss Neil and his mates off in 4,000 years-time we'll not include an information board."

This momentous discovery captured the imagination of archaeologists and was reported about extensively in the Eastern Daily Press and yet it hardly created a rustle in the pages of the tabloid newspapers, proving the shamefully scant attention typically paid by the 'nationals' to this geographically remote and astonishing area.

Here's another instance for you, to prove my point…

I've mentioned before, you can be strolling about in this neck of the woods and never know what you may come across. In May 2013, Nicholas Ashton (curator at the British Museum) and Martin Bates (from St David's University in Wales) happened to be in Happisburgh carrying out research as part of the 'Pathways to Ancient Britain' project. After a spell of intense stormy weather, soft beach sand and layers of sediment underneath were washed away exposing shallow hollows in the remaining silts. It was a huge stroke of luck that two of the UK's leading experts were walking along the shoreline, as part of their official endeavours, soon after and were able to identify the 'hollows' as possibly being human footprints. I say 'a huge stroke of luck' because if that had been you are I (OK then, me) undertaking an early morning stroll I'd have thought 'Hmmm...those dints look vaguely like some other folks have been down here earlier today' or, more likely, just 'Hmmm...look at those dints' - I wouldn't have twigged or even been the least bit inquisitive. Due to their expertise, Ashton and Bates got the feeling there was a bit more to them though and, after images had been analysed by Isabelle De Groote of Liverpool John Moores University, were confirmed to be a set of fossilized hominid footprints. Dated to the end of the early Pleistocene sub-epoch from around 950,000-850,000 years ago, it made them the oldest ever-known hominid footprints found outside Africa. Before this discovery, that distinction had sat (for Europe) with tracks found at the Roccamonfina volcano in Italy dated to around 350,000 years ago.

There's no doubt that scientists, archaeologists, researchers, analysts and geophysicists went into a frenzy at hearing such news, with some reportedly seen cartwheeling, back-flipping and somersaulting across the land, unable to curb their excitement. A scattering of tourists was also drawn to the coast to see if they could catch a glimpse for themselves. Again, the Eastern Daily Press ran a few articles at the time but, overall, this staggering find didn't light the blue touchpaper leading to the offices of the larger news outlets, with some filing reports in the bargain bucket sections located at the bottom of pages 14 and 15 alongside reports of reality stars getting a new tattoo or lip piercing.

Thank goodness for the information boards, that's all I can say. I just wish there were a lot more of them and that one had been available on Trimingham beach, where we walked during the afternoon, but more about that later…

After Walcott we navigated our way around the gas terminals of Bacton before strolling down the hill and into the pretty Victorian seaside village of Mundesley. Our first port of call was the sizeable, flint-faced Ship Inn, a well-earned pit stop that's roughly halfway between Happisburgh and Overstrand. As Leesh and I hovered outside, ascertaining which door would be the best way to enter the pub, I spotted a couple of blokes who were also about to go in.

We made a dart for it and got to the bar first. I was delighted to see that there were three ales in cask form, these being Woodforde's Wherry, Sharp's Atlantic (4.5% pale ale) and Woodforde's Nelson's Revenge. It was fair to say I was thirsty as I selected a pint of the latter. As the friendly barman began to pull my beer, one of the gents who I'd noticed outside entered, stage right. I sensed trouble was in the air, Mundesley-style.

E-mail Man: "Excuse me my good Sir. I've received

an e-mail from the Ship Inn this morning and want to know where you got my address from."

Bartender: "You must have given us it at some time in the past, otherwise how would we know it?"

E-mail Man: "No. I've never given you that information."

Bartender: "You must have done. We can't magic an e-mail address out of thin air. Have you filled one of our surveys out at some time maybe?"

E-mail Man: "No. I've never filled out a survey from here."

The barman deemed this an opportune moment to stop pulling my beer and dedicate his whole attention to the e-mail issue…for fuck's sake.

Bartender: "Well, you must have supplied your details in some shape or form."

E-mail Man: "No. I've never given you my details."

Bartender: "Could a partner have provided us with the address?"

E-mail Man: "No. My wife would never do such a thing."

With a sigh, the adorable Alisha and I plonked ourselves down at the nearest table, waiting for the most mind-numbingly-boring question and answer session ever to finish, waiting for the dust to settle, waiting for our pints.

Two locals, Chris (of a West Ham persuasion) and Stewart (a Leicester City supporter) were keenly watching proceedings, shaking their heads in unison as they empathised with our difficulties in getting served when we were so obviously in need of refreshments.

Monotonous exchanges continued for what seemed like another 3 hours before *E-mail Man* wrapped things up by arriving at the astute conclusion that he'd "have to unsubscribe if anything like this was ever to happen again." Well, thank goodness for that. Now please do promptly piss off and let me get my beer.

The interior of the Ship Inn had a nautical theme as you would expect, with the walls adorned with oars, a ship's wheel and several paintings of random sailing vessels. Due to the pub's idyllic location 'overlooking the golden sands of Mundesley beach' and age (it's well over 200 years old) I found it relatively easy to imagine the pub as having been a hive for smugglers and other local ne'er-do-well's back in the Georgian era. Nowadays its popular with tourists who enjoy the clean and comfortable 'rooms and suites' and diners taking advantage of the extensive menu.

A good chat was had with Chris and Stewart who, after finding out we were making for Overstrand, gave us the tantalising tip that we should research that village's connection to Winston Churchill - we most certainly would. I opted for a second pint and could quite honestly have stayed all afternoon. I was enjoying the company, savouring the Nelson's Revenge and maybe I had become a little too comfortable, especially as we still had a couple of hours walking to get through in the day...and as we finally left the Ship I was aware that I was feeling a tad fatigued both physically and mentally. Surely I would begin to feel more energetic once exposed to the fresh coastal air again?

Meandering wearily down Beach Road towards the Maritime Museum, it was as though I was stumbling my way home after a good night out. I realised I had the 'munchies' and was delighted to encounter the Lobster Pot, a caravan-type trailer anchored at the very corner of a carpark before Jim's Surf Shack. Now, I'm assuming Leeshy chose her favourite of the largest 'dressed crab' possible and that I plumped for a seafood medley of fish sticks, cockles and whelks but I can't honestly recall with any certainty. I had a strange and off-putting humming sound in my ears, as though surrounded by a thousand bees, and it was clear those couple of pints had puddled the senses in more ways than one. We carried on, heading out of Mundesley and straight through a couple of caravan parks, before emerging at a pathways cross-section where one waymarker teasingly pointed straight into the middle of a tall, prickly hedge while another one tentatively arrowed towards a steep and narrow lane that headed down onto a rather rough-looking shoreline – even from a distance it was evident this wasn't Madeira, Majorca or Mablethorpe for that matter. We were flummoxed. Looking at each other, "not...a...clue" was uttered simultaneously.

"Well, we've got to go one way or the other" I blathered dimly, being as decisive as an Ipswich Town goalkeeper facing an on-target free kick from a Chilean midfielder (if you know, you know). With apprehension we surveyed the tarmac track, locally referred to as 'The Gap', that led down to the beach and it was at this moment that I got the inkling that my daughter was also flagging. "Big lad, if we get to the bottom of THAT, and you decide it's not the correct way to go, I am NOT walking back up."

Dear Reader, you are undoubtedly wondering at this stage, where Phoebe Smith's much thumbed guidebook was and why the hell it wasn't being consulted. Well, I did have a look but, with definitely no fault attributed to that author, I admit I just couldn't make any sense of the simple maps or decipher the undemanding and very clear text – yet a choice still had to be made. "It's got to be along the beach" I decided and down 'The Gap' we went.

Playing on the secluded stretch of sand was a youthful chap (and the only person I could see) who had his extremely energetic border collie tearing about after a yellow tennis ball. As we approached them, the dog scampered up to his human and plopped the retrieved object at his foot before sitting attentively at his side, eyes obsessively focussed on his toy and panting profusely. Meanwhile, tired and slightly dismayed it has to be said, I looked up at the looming cliffs and instantly knew I'd chosen incorrectly.

After hurling the ball once more into the distance, I asked the young fellow if it was possible to reach our destination by walking along the beach and, more to the point, was it safe to do so. He confirmed that it was on both counts before adding "I was on my way there myself. But I noticed, in the distance, a couple with at least six dogs and I wasn't sure they were on leads or not" – I assumed he was talking about the dogs and not the couple. "I didn't want to take the risk and get into an altercation, that's the only reason I turned back. As you walk along yourself you will see them. They will have walked from Overstrand." He then gesticulated towards the sea and continued "Plus, you can see for yourself that the tide is on its way out" and with that we commenced walking along Trimingham Beach, albeit with an air of trepidation.

The first hundred metres or so are not too bad, similar to many other stretches along this part of the coast. There are the familiar crumbling cliffs as a backdrop, the typically bedraggled sea defence in situ, soft sand landside before becoming harder towards the outgoing tide, a scattering of flint and pebbles dotted about with opportunistic birds swooping down to get a closer look at what may be in the left-behind rock pools. However, after this calm and normal stretch you stroll around a bend and are alarmingly transported through a portal into a different world.

You know when you approach an inner city 'estate' pub, let's say in one of the more spiky and potentially challenging areas in the suburbs of Sheffield, Liverpool or Manchester for example? From the outside the building doesn't look like it is hoarding many perils so you are lulled into thinking 'Yeah, I'll pop in here for one. How rough can it be'? Once through the door your trainers immediately stick to the carpet and you realise you may have miscalculated as you spot handwritten signs advertising forthcoming sponsored cock-fighting events and bare-knuckle scraps, all proceeds kindly donated to the local hospice, of course. Karaoke is in full flow at half eleven in the morning and then, before you get the chance to order a pint of Skol or Ayingerbrau lager (or whatever it is they dispense in these establishments), you are approached by a local 'character' asking if you're interested in purchasing a pack of razor blades, or a freshly caught trout, or a pair of size 14 fluffy slippers. Politely declining the chance of buying any of these delightful items, said local 'character' suddenly turns feisty and berates you because 'you're doing nothing for the local economy'. You look around for support only to catch the eye of a toothless woman, with more make-up caked on her face than a fallen B movie actress. She gives you a suggestive nod and a wink. In effect, you're out of your comfort zone but, now you're in there you've got to go ahead with it and select your drink, there's no turning back now. Well, it reminded me of that scenario.

Those eroding crags were taller and more intimidating than we'd seen before and yet conversely appeared flimsier, with water slowly but insistently seeping out and downwards, spasmodically forcing off huge slabs of mud and clay as it did so. The sea defences here were more dilapidated with the resultant debris of wood, metal and chunks of concrete strewn all over. It was carnage and, believe it or not, much worse than the walk down Princes Street/Portman Road from a railway station in a certain Suffolk town. Being hemmed in between the cliffs and what remained of the sea wall/revetments (barricades) did make the temperature feel extravagantly warm but this was not a place for parasols, sunbeds, inflatables or beach-side bars dispensing ice-cold beers. This was total desolation. Then we came upon an old, ruined, narrow gauge railway line – and yes, you've read that correctly. An old, ruined, narrow gauge railway line…

Locally there are three 'trains' of thought as to what its purpose was. The most common one is that, after World War II, the track was laid to aid mine and bomb disposal. The unexploded devices were collected and then ever-so-carefully transported along the line to areas of the beach where controlled explosions could take place safely. This may be true as it does appear that several 'bombs have been dropped' along this shoreline. However, I'm not totally convinced of this explanation. I've observed one photograph of the working railway, admittedly a grainy black and white one, where the engine is pulling half a dozen 'tubs' along behind it, similar in shape to what we see present day freight trains heaving along, the type that contain limestone chippings or coal for example. Surely if you were retrieving UXBs you would only be taking one at a time for safety reasons, therefore requiring just the one container, or two at most? It is possible, of course, that I have gone 'off track' with my logic here.

Secondly, there's a possibility that it was laid to assist with the urgent construction of sea defences after the devastating floods to the area of 1953 (where 1,500 square acres of land were inundated resulting in the deaths of over 300 people, with 30,000 being evacuated). I wouldn't necessarily want to 'rail against' this idea, with those 'tubs' looking likelier to be utilised for carrying the necessary commodities to build the required barricade.

The final word surely has to go with the local experts, especially the people responsible for the extremely informative website 'Trimingham.org'. Under a section headed *'Construction of the Trimingham Revetments'* can be found the following clarification: *'1974 A construction railway was positioned behind the concrete and wooden defences as they were being built. Multiple cliff collapses left equipment damaged and forced the abandonment of sections of track, some of which can still be seen when the tide has scoured behind the defences'.*

Now, I don't think for one moment that they have 'hit the buffers' with this description but, all I'm saying is, I'd love to see an official information board in the location detailing this. That really would be the 'end of the line' for me…

Onwards we trudged, clambering over more slabs

of concrete, sections of upended iron railway track/sleepers, planks of wood, house bricks, flint and the husk of an old, discarded lorry cab that still had shredded rubber tyres, just about, attached to rusting wheels. We'd passed the couple with the six dogs (they were on leads) but other than them we didn't see another soul.

The gooey slabs of mud and clay, discarded from higher up on the cliff face, were proving to be an ongoing hindrance as the trickling, narrow channels of fresh water continued to chip away at the surface as it oozed downwards. Mistakenly, I'd always thought coastal erosion was solely related to the constant pounding by the sea and that man-made barricades were the only means of prevention. I'd not considered, for one moment, that there may be another reason with another remedy. I'll leave it to Liz King, chairman of Trimingham parish council, to provide the following explanation:

'We're looking at a project moving forward to seed the whole of the cliff so that it binds together and absorbs an awful lot of that water, because it's not the sea but the water coming off the land which is eroding the cliff away. What we're trying to do is use that water before it takes the cliff away. Years ago there were hundreds of wells in the village as every property had its own well which were drawing up and using water. We've also tried using pipes to drain water out of the cliffs. Now we've been talking to a company about the possibility of using drones – with about a five-foot span – to drop seeds over the cliffs'.

Sounds like a good plan yet, as homes continue to perish, it doesn't need me to point out that time is of the essence.

Eventually, after what seemed an eternity, we spotted the steep set of steps leading up into Overstrand. Coming at the tail end of 3 days of rambling, I don't mind admitting that I'd found that final haul along the beach quite tough. I was tired, thirsty, sweaty and my hamstrings were as taut as finely tuned piano strings. However, as we began to walk down the High Street with its appealingly idiosyncratic buildings, I realised with an outpouring of pride that this was it, we'd (just about) completed the Norfolk Coast Path in its entirety. An overwhelming and glowing feeling gushed over me, that it had all been worth it, that we'd done something special. Agreed, we still had a couple of steady miles to accomplish along the cliffs the following morning to get to Cromer, but this had all the makings of approaching the last few metres of an official long-distance event, with the finishing line for us being the tantalising entrance into the White Horse pub. As with the start of the walk all those months ago back in

Hunstanton, there was no fanfare to herald our arrival, no brass band playing and no official figure rushing over to place medals around our necks, but we knew what we'd achieved...and before we stepped through the door into the pub, and with a huge smile covering my face, I gave my daughter, the adorable Alisha, a big old embrace. "Stop being soft, big lad and get yourself to the bar. It's your round" she said.

Located centrally in this quaint village, the White Horse is a lively place. It provides all the things that you'd expect a traditional type of pub to do including real ales, lagers and ever-popular gins, a games room with pool table, Sky and BT coverage in the bar for those popular sporting events and to the rear there's a lawned beer garden with a shaded patio. You can see the interior has been knocked about a bit in recent times with the ground floor rooms now featuring clean modern lines, housing subtle but sophisticated mis-matched furniture, as is the current trend. Breakfast, lunch and dinner is served daily, while upstairs there are ten individually styled en suite rooms available. Leesh and I would be having an evening meal, staying overnight, and, of course, drinking here.

We received a lovely welcome from Lucy who not only checked us in but perceptively served us a beer before doing so. I selected a pint of Little Sharpie for starters, a refreshing 3.8% golden session bitter from the Humpty Dumpty brewery located 35 miles down the road in Reedham. Four other cask beers were available, these being Grain Oak (another 3.8% easy drinking golden bitter) and then three from Greene King that I hadn't encountered previously: Fresh Legs (4% golden ale), Bonkers Conkers (4.1% brown ale) and Mischief Maker (6% double dry hopped IPA). Purely to aid the crucial process of rehydration, a couple of pints were swiftly necked before we retired to our room for rejuvenating showers and a grateful change of clothing. I'm not saying I stunk but I had noticed, on the walk through Overstrand, the hedgerows wilting as I brushed past.

"Enough of that Neil!" I hear you exclaim. "It's high time you told us about Winston Churchill and what he was doing in the village all those years ago." I knew this was coming, and there's no need to thank me but on your behalf, I have indeed done some research. Are you sitting comfortably? Good. Then I'll begin...

The story starts to take shape in 1883 when London journalist and travel writer Clement Scott, visited Overstrand and lodged at the Mill House with local miller Alfred Jermy and his daughter Louie (rumour had it he'd planned to stay in Cromer but there were no vacancies). He adored the place so much that he penned several romanticised and extremely well-received articles, mainly for the Daily Telegraph, christening the area 'Poppyland' - an endearing term that caught the imagination of his esteemed and affluent readers.

When land for development came on the market, the village magnetically attracted some of the richest people in the land such as bankers, lawyers and politicians, all wealthy, cultured and proficient in well-connected social circles. The clincher, for these people, was that Overstrand was considered by them to be 'not as common' as near neighbour Cromer.

At the peak of its popularity numerous millionaires resided there, including Cyril Flower (who was soon to become Lord Battersea), Lord Hillingdon (a partner in Glyn, Mills & Company bank), Sir Edgar Speyer (financier and future chairman of the London Underground), Sir William Player (tobacco magnate) and Sir Jesse Boot (of pharmaceutical giant, Boots the Chemist). Also appearing periodically with their buckets and spades were Sir Frederick Macmillan (son of the founder of the publishing empire), Edward Lyttelton (headmaster of Eton) and classicist Gilbert Murray. All these people had a taste for the finer things in life and, without a doubt, didn't hesitate in spending their riches to obtain them. For instance, rising young architect

Edwin Lutyens was head-hunted to design, plan and supervise the buildings of The Pleasaunce and Overstrand Hall for Lords Battersea and Hillingdon respectively. You can see why Overstrand quickly acquired the moniker 'Village of Millionaires'.

Other celebrated visitors flocked to stay with such opulent hosts. This was the seaside place to be. Queen Alexandra frequented the Hillingdon's, Sidney and Beatrice Webb (co-founders of the London School of Economics and Political Science) kipped at the Battersea's while, and here's the moment you've been waiting for, Lady Randolph Churchill accompanied by her sons Winston and Jack, frequently bunked up with the Speyer's at what is now known as the Sea Marge Hotel – I'd walked past this building earlier and instantly imagined Agatha Christie's Miss Marple busily flitting from room to room attempting to solve a murder.

Fast forward a few years and Winston, now married to Clementine, was also holidaying in Overstrand with his own young family. In the summer of 1914, with the World War I on the horizon, his wife was determined that their kids, Diana and Randolph, should have a vacation and that her husband join them for some rest and relaxation from his demanding admiralty duties. Joined by Winston's brother Jack and his family two cottages were rented, with Clementine selecting Pear Tree for her brood while the other Churchills chose Beckhithe that was at the opposite end of the lawn.

On Sunday 26th July 1914, in what must have been one of the most momentous telephone calls of the time, Winston spoke with Prince Louis of Battenberg (the First Sea Lord) and decided there and then that events demanded his presence. He left Overstrand, returning to London on the admiralty yacht HMS Enchantress, and a couple of weeks later, at 11 o'clock on the night of the 4th of August, Great Britain was at war with Germany.

I do not know if Churchill ever returned after the end of the global conflict. It is widely acknowledged though that by 1919 the general obsession with Poppyland by 'distinctly superior people' – a term coined within a 1903 court circular – was all but over. The 'Village of Millionaires' label was no longer applicable as the rich and famous either moved on or passed away and by the mid-1930's most of the grand houses had been converted into hotels, nursing homes or apartments.

I'm not insinuating for one moment that present day residents of Overstrand are impoverished, far from it. In fact, Leesh and I had already mentioned what an exceptional village it was; from the outside looking in, the attractive houses were in excellent condition with gardens well maintained. You still needed a sovereign or two to live here.

Freshly showered, suitably rested and sporting a refreshing change of clobber we returned to the bar. I wasn't messing about on what was to be our last (and celebratory) evening and immediately ordered a pint of the 6% Mischief Maker. Amiable and chatty local Reginald was already in attendance and quickly struck up a conversation with us, asking the usual stuff about what we were doing in the area, were we having a nice time and what did we think to Overstrand. I commented about how well it all looked and that there was an obvious air of affluence encompassing it. He nodded in agreement and began to tell us a tale about a 'very well off' good mate of his called Jasper.

Now, the story goes that Jasper stepped outside the front door of his palatial residence one morning and, for some reason, looked up at the ceiling of his porch and recognised that it required a lick of paint. As you'd imagine, it wasn't the normal- sized porch that you'd see on the front of a suburban semi; this was one of those that wrapped around part of the building, sheltering and shading strategically placed tables and chairs used for chilling-out, enjoying an early-morning cafetiere of coffee, having an early-evening carafe of chablis, that sort of thing. Anyway, he decided to enlist the services of 'Handyman Harry', an endearing character well known to him, and others in the area, for being a jack of all trades while perhaps not being able to master most of them. It was also fair to add that there were definitely sharper tools to be found in his box. Jasper instructed 'Handyman Harry' that he would provide the materials and all he wanted him to do was paint the porch. Jasper then went off to Holt for a business meeting before returning later in the afternoon, eager to inspect the odd-job-man's work.

'Handyman Harry' was waiting for him by the elaborate wrought iron gates at the head of the driveway. "Job done Mr Jasper." he said. "There was quite a lot of paint left over so I've given it two good coats." Jasper, very impressed, reached into his pocket and took out a wad of notes in order to pay. "By the way" added the handyman "that's not a Porch you've got, it's a Lamborghini."

True story that.

At the White Horse I'd read that the head chef and team were passionate about producing as much food as possible from their kitchen where breads were baked, fish was smoked and ice-cream churned. They placed a big emphasis on local produce with lobsters from Overstrand, crabs from Cromer and marsh samphire from the area's saltmarshes all favoured, when in season. I'd seen the menu and everything looked extremely appetising but could the team deliver the goods? Our selections were:

Leesh – Cromer crab and Sheringham smoked salmon fishcake, poached egg, hollandaise sauce, skinny fries & a side salad.

Me – Garlic and paprika marinated pork ribeye, chorizo, new potato patatas bravas & Norfolk asparagus.

I'm delighted to say the meals were excellent. A cacophony of sensual tastes, as someone may once have said, and a fitting way to round off a memorable day and wonderful evening.

Day 8 miles walked: 13.03 / Total miles walked: 98.86

OVERSTRAND TO CROMER

'H mmm...not sure I can be arsed to walk to Cromer this morning' I mused on waking up. 'I'll casually suggest to Leesh that I've thought of a wonderful opportunity where we can catch a bus, or even call a taxi straight to the railway station. She'll be happy with that'. It was time to head home to Chesterfield but the previous evening's enthusiastic imbibing of copious amounts of Mischief Maker had naughtily created a thick head. My aching muscles were also critically informing me that they didn't have much left in the tank and I was feeling frail. In my favour I'd noted my daughter mention, during the trek along Trimingham Beach, that her Achilles tendons were tight and causing her some grief. Maybe she'd prefer a lift anyway?

"No thanks Dad. I've walked the whole path so far and I'm not going to miss out on the last two and a half miles. You can do what you want but I'm walking it. Have a couple of paracetamols and get some water down you. You'll be alright."

Bugger. Worth a try though.

Against my better judgement I accompanied her down to breakfast where we were the first ones into the dining room. I had a tentative sniff around the cereals, fresh fruits and breads but unsurprisingly nothing took my fancy. Slightly sweating, I necked several refreshing glasses of iced water and envied Alisha as she began to tuck into her full English. Even though I felt rough, I could still appreciate the quality of ingredients and how they had been well cooked and conscientiously presented on the plate. "You're missing a real treat here big lad" she taunted as she caught my eye, licking her lips as she spurted on some brown sauce.

Our breakfast party of two was then bolstered by a forceful young chappie who bellowed out "GOOD MORNING!" a little too loudly for my liking as he boisterously entered the room. He had a distinctive look about him, exhibiting a well-manicured band of facial hair across his upper lip. I'm sure I'd read somewhere that, in this day and age, if we came across a male sporting a moustache we should recognise that this person was indeed lost and needed to be returned instantly to Ipswich but, then again, he could have grown it for a bet I guess.

Without a doubt, he was a clatterer of the first order. Cereal bowls clanged, fruit dishes clanked and glasses clinked while spoons were tapped furiously on the side of anything he could set his sights on, like a demented percussionist from a thrash metal band.

The din was too much for me. "I'm going up to finish packing my bag" I whispered to Leesh. "See you in a bit."

"HAVE A GREAT DAY MATE!" boomed the moustachioed reverberator.

"You too you noisy fucker" I thought, as I slithered out of the room, desperately seeking sanctuary.

It wasn't too long afterwards that we checked out of the White Horse and were heading down Cliff Road towards...yep, you've guessed correctly, the cliff. The North Sea, our constant companion these last few days, was calmness personified down to our right, with waves gently lapping forwards onto the beach before retreating back in a visible change of mind. The early morning chill kept me on my toes as we skirted along the extremity of the local golf course, with the enchanting beam from the lighthouse rotating around to check on our progress every 4, or was it 5, maybe even 6 seconds. "Stop gawping at that light Dad and concentrate on the path. I don't want you falling over the cliff" wisely advised my ever-alert daughter.

Reaching the outskirts of Cromer we began to descend into the town down a gently sloping and well-maintained path. It was here we came across the memorial bust of the one and only Henry Blogg. 'Who's that then Neil', I hear you ask? Well, thanks for enquiring.

Henry George Blogg (1876–1954) was a member of the Cromer section of the Royal National Lifeboat Institution (RNLI) and became the most decorated in their history. In an organization teeming with heroically brave volunteers, I'm sure you'll appreciate that is quite an accomplishment. I've mentioned the lifeboatmen in glowing terms before (when we were walking through Caister) but I think he warrants a special mention. Simply referred to as '*the greatest of the lifeboatmen*' here is his story, with some of his outstanding achievements…

Henry initially joined up with his local crew in 1894 becoming the coxswain 15 years later, a position he retained for 38 years until retirement in 1947. In that time he took part in a mammoth 387 rescues, helping to save a truly remarkable 873 lives. They say 'superheroes wear capes' but this one was more likely to be found wearing a hand-knitted gansey, oilskins and a sou'wester. His first rescue to capture the imagination occurred in 1917 when his crew launched their lifeboat *'Louisa Heartwell'* four times within 14 hours during a terrible storm. Battling severe winds they successfully rescued the 22 members who were onboard the stricken Greek vessel *'Pyrin'*. Relying on 14 oars and 2 sails to navigate the heavy seas Henry's crew, that day, had an average age of over 50 years with two of them being over 70. Triumphant yet exhausted they arrived back on shore only to be notified that they were required to instantly return to sea as the Swedish ship *'Fernabo'* had been blown in two by a naval mine. On this occasion, they rowed out three times in attempting to save the onboard sailors. Henry was awarded his first gold medal for his efforts and was commended for his 'remarkable personality and admirable leadership'. His crew received bronze medals and were lauded for their 'courage and dogged tenacity'.

Moving forward a few years to 1932, the Italian vessel *'Monte Nevoso'* ran aground on the Haisborough Sands. Cromer's lifeboat was launched along with several tugs in a valiant attempt to refloat the ship but unfortunately it began to break up. As the crew were taken to safety the officers refused to leave. A determined Henry returned twice to try to coax them off but on that second visit found that they had abandoned ship, leaving behind a Tyrolean mountain dog and numerous caged birds (which were all saved). By the time they returned home, Henry and his team had been at sea for a monumental 52 hours. He was awarded a silver medal for his endeavours and praised for his 'faultless seamanship, great courage and endurance'. As a show of gratitude he was gifted the dog who he renamed Monte.

In 1935, Cromer lifeboat station received delivery of a motor-powered craft named 'H.F. Bailey'. In a call out to the 'SS English Trader' in 1941, aground on Hammond's Knoll off Happisburgh, disaster was narrowly averted after the 'H.F. Bailey' rolled onto her side. Five crew members were thrown into the water with Henry being one of them. William H Davies, still onboard, grasped hold of the wheel and steered the corrected lifeboat towards his flailing colleagues. One by one they were saved although Walter Allen would not survive for long due to a failing heart. Henry directed the lifeboat from the 'SS English Trader' and headed for the nearest safe haven at Great Yarmouth. At 3 o'clock the next morning he woke his crew, ready to try again and they were soon back at the sands. By now the rough seas had abated sufficiently enough for 44 men to be rescued, none of whom had expected to live through the night. Henry was presented with the RNLI silver medal for his efforts with the rest of the men receiving bronze ones, Walter Allen posthumously.

Amongst a whole host of accolades, Henry Blogg was awarded the gold medal of the RNLI three times, the silver medal four times, the George Cross, the Empire Gallantry Medal and the British Empire Medal. He was even presented with a silver medal by the Canine Defence League for saving Monte. At the bottom of his memorial bust are inscribed the words 'ONE OF THE BRAVEST MEN WHO EVER LIVED'.

...and here's me harping on about feeling under the weather due to an alcohol induced hangover.

We carried on further down the hill until stopping outside the Red Lion. This seemed an ideal place for a final celebratory photo, the elevated position containing two beaming, triumphant walkers blessed with having the iconic pier and surrounding might of the sea as the perfect backdrop. Our quest to walk the entirety of the Norfolk Coast Path had officially been achieved.

Essential provisions for the train journey home were sought from the 'High Street's Co-op', including cans of ale, multipacks of crisps and, needless to say, the Norwich Evening News. A lady with mental health issues was causing mayhem in the store, calling male shoppers 'nonces' and 'faggots' while the women were either 'sluts' or 'slags'. She ordered everyone to keep their distance from her as she didn't want to be 'contaminated' by any of us. We were more than happy to oblige although I'm sure I wasn't the only one who realised this wasn't personal and that she desperately needed help.

With the uncomfortable shopping experience over, we sauntered up towards the rail station and passed by the 'Chesterfield Villas' in order to catch our train home, via Norwich. I wondered if the row of houses enjoyed any link with my hometown, or if they had been named after a large couch with rolled arms that are the same height as the back (often upholstered in a dark leather, with deep button tufting all over and a nail head trim), or christened after a brand of cigarettes that contained an original blend of Turkish and Virginia tobacco. Well, it was nothing to do with any of these. The properties were built in the 1800s by John and Margaret Bond Cabbell, who owned Cromer Hall. John also had a home in London, situated at 1 Chesterfield Gardens (built on land owned by the Earl of Chesterfield), and he named the villas after this address. Not the most exhilarating of explanations I must admit, but there you have it.

We enjoyed a pleasantly uneventful journey into Norwich rail station, arriving in good time to catch our onwards connection home. The much-maligned Liverpool Lime Street to Norwich train service (which we were to take in the opposite direction) had been discussed recently in the House of Lords with Lord Birt stating that, if you so desired, you would be able to fly from Liverpool to Egypt in a quicker time than the 5 and a half hours taken for the rail journey. I appreciate the point he was trying to make although it's slightly unfair to compare the performance of an antiquated rattler with that of a sleek, narrow-bodied airliner. Plus, he's missing the main point here, isn't he? Why would anyone prefer to take a flight to the north-east corner of Africa (although I'm sure it's very pleasant once you get there) when a train can be taken towards the north-east corner of East Anglia and you can delight in all the special, unique pleasures that area has to offer. After all, if anywhere exceptional is worth visiting there always appears to be an inordinate amount of time and energy needed to get you there in the first place. The adorable Alisha and I had enjoyed such a wonderful time along the whole route that all the planning and subsequent exertions had made it all seem worthwhile. We'd rambled through saltmarshes, along cliffs, trader trails, beaches, fields and copses, sauntered through picturesque towns and villages and quaffed quality local ales and ciders in some superb hostelries...plus, we'd also raised a 'bob or two' for charity. This had been a truly enjoyable and fruitful experience with treasured memories to last a lifetime.

The rail journey home was punctual, comfortable and relaxed, some would say just as it should be. There was no spontaneous cabaret this time, no fancy dress and no train manager taking centre stage. As I drained the remaining dregs out of my last can of alcoholic beverage, the fields and hedgerows had fallen by the wayside as we energetically swept through the Chesterfield suburbs of Tupton, wi' Wingerworth on one side o'tracks, Grassmoor on t'other then finally Hasland, with its terrace houses proudly lining the route to herald our return. The Alma Leisure Park came into view, the unofficial 'locals' sign of arrival for us to stiffly prise ourselves from the seats, gather our bags and then step down onto the platform after the train, with a slight jolt, gasped to a halt.

In an instant Chesterfield was seeping back into my bones, this familiar and well frequented station its usual hive of activity with corporate workers fretting vociferously into their mobile phones as laid-back leisure travellers secretly and smugly commiserated with their plight. Outside the sun shone brightly as we adeptly sidestepped a drunken punter who was aggressively threatening to punch the lights out of a bemused-looking taxi driver. Business as usual then in the everyday life of this north Derbyshire ex-mining town.

The statue of George Stephenson, middle finger and all, remained in his custodial and proud position, surveying the short stay car park where the delectable Denise was waiting to give us a welcome lift.

"Gerra move on you two…I think that traffic warden's coming over to gi' me a bloody ticket!" she said. With a warm glow, I surely knew we were now back on home ground, the definitive start and end of our ramble along the beautiful Norfolk Coast Path.

Day 9 miles walked: 2.24 / Total miles walked: 101.10

THE REAL ALE RAMBLER ROLL OF HONOUR

Bannister, Robert – Publisher. In fact, my favourite Publisher (although I do only know the one).

Bristow, Richard of *Norfolk Pubs* website.

Hardy, Gregg – Cover Artist. Extremely talented Caricaturist. Drinking Buddy.

Jones, Caroline –Expert on the Iron Duke and all things Great Yarmouth. A force of nature.

Newspapers – *Eastern Daily Press, Norwich Evening News* and *Great Yarmouth Mercury*. Valuable resources for all things Norfolk.

Pennycook, Carol – All round Good Egg. Stepped into the breach when we had nowhere to stay.

Radford, Chris (and all at *Brampton Brewery, Chesterfield*) – Generous supporter(s) of the book. I remain forever grateful.

Self, Cameron of *Literary Norfolk* website.

Smith, Phoebe – Our Tour Guide and revered 'Wander Woman'. Author of *Walking the Peddars Way and Norfolk Coast Path*.

Stradling, Rod of *Mustrad* website.

Village, Trimingham – There are towns and cities that don't have a website as comprehensive and informative as *Trimingham.org.*

Wigfield, Paula – Proof Reader. Mrs Motivator and Grammatical Guru. "Neil, what's happening with all these commas?"

…and last but by no means least, my **Family** – The delectable Denise, The pristine Paige and The adorable Alisha. Always there for me, even if they are sometimes a bit late.

"Control the controllables and leave the rest to sort themselves out."

THE REAL ALE
RAMBLER

QUAFFING ALONG THE NORFOLK COAST PATH

NEIL COLLINGS

Cheers!

Neil Collings